OUTLINES FOR JUNIOR ASSEMBLIES

'TRICIA WILLIAMS

Scripture Union

© 'Tricia Williams 1996

First published 1996

Scripture Union, 207-209 Queensway, Milton Keynes, Bletchley, MK2 2EB, England.

ISBN 1 85999 040 1

British Library Cataloguing-in-Publication Data.
A catalogue record of this book is available from the British Library.

Design and illustration by Patricia Donnelly Graphic Design.
Printed and bound in Great Britain by Ebenezer Baylis.

CONTENTS

Introduction   7
Using this book   12

Section I Everyone matters   21
You're special
1   How much are you worth?   22
2   The lost sheep   24
3   Don't forget your toothbrush!   31
Living with others
4   The untouchables   33
5   Do what's right   35
6   We need each other   37
7   The carpenter's tools   39
8   Rules for life   45

Section II God and me   48
9   God knows how you feel   49
10 Getting rid of your rubbish   50
11 Take your pick   53
12 Choose life   56
13 Do what it says   58
14 Listening   60
15 Talk to God – he's listening   62
16 God made me   65
17 God's got plans for you   67
18 How to be a frog   71
19 Secrets   74
20 Record breakers!   80
21 I can't!   82

Section III Meet Jesus 85

22 Meet Jesus! 86

23 Forgiveness 89

24 The price is right 92

25 Mission impossible 93

26 You are invited 95

27 Mistakes 98

28 Bad news ... good news 102

29 Try it and see 104

Section IV Special Occasions 107

Harvest 108

30 Loaves and fishes 108

Remembrance Day 111

31 Heroes 111

Christmas 113

32 Jesus – God's gift to you 113

33 Happy birthday, Jesus! 115

34 The best present 120

New Year 122

35 New Year drawer 122

36 A New Year's revolution 124

Lent 127

37 Recipe for ... pancakes! 127

38 Give me strength! 130

Easter 133

39 Crosses 133

40 Breakfast on the beach 136

Pentecost 138

41 How does he do that? 138

End of year 141

42 All change 141

Further resources and useful addresses 144

LIST OF CONTRIBUTORS AND ACKNOWLEDGEMENTS

Linda Anderson (3, 8, 11, 37)
Esther Bailey (5, 9, 17, 23, 25)
Joanna Bailey (4, 24, 41)
Simon Barker (6, 10)
Steve Bullock (16, 31, 32, 39)
Claire Derry (1, 40 and song suggestions)
Wayne Dixon (2)
Helen Franklin (13, 27, 28)
Nick Harding (14)
Gill Hutchinson (song suggestions)
Graham Jones (12)
John Marshall (7)
Alison Mitchell (15, 22, 33)
Jeannie Poulton (38)
Andy Saunders (26)
Jane Smith (20, 21)
John Stephenson (36)
Ian Vallance (18, 19)
Helen Venables (30, 34, 35, 42)
'Tricia Williams (introduction and additional material)

The idea for 29 *Try it and see* was taken from *On Track*, a Scripture Union in Schools publication*.

Many thanks to Jan Wilkinson for reading the material and for her helpful comments.

* *On Track*, Scripture Union in Schools, September 1994.
  On Track magazine is published in-house, termly, and is available on subscription.

INTRODUCTION

Time and space for God

For many children assembly is the only time and space they have to think about God and his relevance to them. The statutory requirement in England and Wales* – that all maintained schools have daily acts of worship, the majority of which are 'wholly or mainly of a broadly Christian character' – provides an opportunity to help children begin to see beyond the values of a material world and to develop an awareness of God – who is there, who cares about them and who has given us guidelines to help us live together.

This book is intended as a resource for all those who want, and are able, to take up that opportunity by leading assemblies for the 7–11 age group in primary schools – as a teacher or a visitor to school. All the outlines in this book are specifically Christian in nature.

If you're a teacher ...

Perhaps you've just seen your own children off to school, battled through the morning traffic and are in the process of

---

* In Scotland the requirement for primary schools is that religious observance, which is broadly Christian in character, takes place at least once a week.

  In Northern Ireland the requirement for grant-aided schools is a daily act of collective worship.

grabbing a quick cup of coffee in the staffroom whilst getting your thoughts together for the day in the classroom. Outside, the children are already in the playground waiting for the whistle. The Head breezes in, glances at the notice-board and says to you, 'You're doing assembly this morning, aren't you?'

You'd forgotten! And now you are due in the classroom to take the register, the dinner money, the trip money, introduce the student who is with your class for the next few weeks, sort out an ongoing dispute about marbles ... and then it's assembly.

Maybe this scenario isn't familiar to you, but for many teachers the responsibility of leading assembly in an already over-crowded day is one thing they could do without, whatever their own personal faith and beliefs. In the context of school, the thirty or so children in your class and their education are your top priority. Assembly feels as if it comes much further down the list. Whatever your ideals, it may help to spend some time deliberately considering the significance of the fact that for many children, school assembly is one of the few places where they hear about God.

This book is not intended to be picked up five minutes before you take an assembly as you hunt – panic-stricken – for an idea! But it is hoped that, as you cope with the many other demands of the school day, these outlines will help you prepare and lead lively, enjoyable assemblies which contribute to the spiritual growth and awareness of the children in your care.

If you're a visitor ...

Remember you are a visitor to the school – a guest. Maybe you were responsible for making contact, but it is the school who has taken up your offer and invited you. Be a wise and courteous guest. That way you might be invited back!

• If you don't already know, find out some background information about the school and what usually happens in assembly:
   • What are the social and ethnic backgrounds of the children?
   • What other faiths, apart from Christian, are represented in the school?

- Are assemblies in the school usually Christian in character?
- What are staff and children used to in assembly (prayer, Bible reading, singing)?

- Check the amount of time you have for the assembly. Keep to those time limits. Order is very important in a school, where staff have the job of caring for a large number of children. Teachers also have a full day and will want to keep to their planned schedules.

- Be punctual. Allow plenty of time if you need to set up equipment or props in the hall before the assembly begins.

- Be flexible. Schools don't always run like clockwork. If someone has forgotten that you were coming, or that half the children would be on a school trip, or that the OHP was stolen in the break-in last week – don't panic, but do be prepared.

- Prepare your assembly well. The school is placing their trust in you in allowing you to lead an assembly.

- Dress in a way which won't draw unhelpful attention to yourself. You want the children (and staff) to be talking at break-time about the content of the assembly, not about the clothes you were wearing (unless they were a deliberate part of the assembly)!

- During the assembly, don't over-excite the children. If they do get excited, make sure you include a calming down slot as well. Remember that teachers have to help them settle to class-room work afterwards.

- If you make any kind of mess in the assembly (paper on the floor, food spilt etc), offer to clear up afterwards.

- Remember that this is a school assembly – not a family service at church or Sunday school. Remember the diverse backgrounds of the children; the fact that most of them will have no involvement with a church; and the responsibility of the school towards the children – to educate, not indoctrinate.

- Remember that your presentation of Christian truth is part of a wider picture. There are others who regularly lead assemblies and there will be children from Christian families who unconsciously communicate Christian values. Religious Education is part of the curriculum and there may be a Christian group functioning in the school. All these different aspects are bringing the reality of God into the life of the school community.

• Ideally, it will be possible for you to take more than one assembly. With regular involvement you can begin to build up a relationship with the children and the staff of the school.

The children

• The children facing you in an assembly come from a wide variety of family situations and social, ethnic and religious backgrounds. Be aware of this as you prepare your material.

• Don't assume knowledge of the Christian faith. Don't put words of belief or commitment into the mouths of children who will want to please you but don't fully understand the meaning of those words. Be respectful of the feelings of the parents of children who hold different faiths, even though you may not agree with their beliefs.

• Most seven to eleven year olds inhabit a world of literal concepts. Avoid abstract ideas and concepts. This can be difficult when it comes to talking about spiritual issues. So, if you need to use abstract words and ideas, make sure you explain them. For example, loving others (in the context of school) means being kind to others, helping, sharing, befriending the lonely. Or give examples of everyday situations to illustrate what you mean.

• Children of this age are looking for safe boundaries and a framework for their lives which makes sense. Absolutes may not be clear for them or for many of their parents.

• Children of this age are inquisitive in an open and non-critical way. They are simply eager to discover and understand more about their world ('How do we know God isn't a lie?' 'Where is heaven?' 'Why doesn't God stop wars happening?'). Make use of this straightforward curiosity, making it clear, where appropriate, when something is your personal belief or what Christians believe.

• Seven to eleven year olds tend to be very trusting of adults – especially any who appear to be in a position of responsibility, like taking an assembly ('But my teacher said so, Mum, so it must be true ...'). Make sure what you tell them is trustworthy and true.

• Children of this age enjoy talking and hearing about their immediate world: their families, school, friends in their street, children's TV, the latest hobbies, games, books, films, music etc. Use illustrations from their world to help the children understand what you want to communicate through the assembly. Watch some children's TV and read some magazines for this age group to get yourself in tune.

• Children enjoy laughing. Use humour in your illustrations (but be careful not to make a child in the assembly a figure of fun).

* *International Children's Bible*, Nelson Word.

USING THIS BOOK

Aim

At the beginning of each assembly outline there is an aim. This is intended to be a helpful summary of the truth or ideas the assembly is trying to communicate to the children. Hold this aim in your mind as you are leading the assembly to help you stay on track. If nothing else, you want the children to go away knowing what the one or two points are that you set out to communicate.

Bible base

Bible passages and verses are given under this heading in many of the outlines. It is not necessarily intended that you refer to these verses directly in the assembly. They may be the references for a story that you have to retell in your own words, or simply background information/teaching which is relevant to the topic of the assembly.

You will need

Nearly all the assembly outlines need a variety of props and equipment. Mostly they are things which you can obtain easily.

Often an overhead projector, acetates and pens are necessary. If so, check whether the school is willing to let you use their OHP and screen. If there isn't one easily available, a flip-chart or large pieces of card or paper can often take the place of an OHP.

Do check the 'You will need' list several days before you take the assembly to make sure you have everything ready. Then, if not, you will still have time to get it.

Preparation

• All the assembly outlines in this book require advance preparation and forethought. It is hoped that the layout of the material makes it easy to understand, memorise and use.

• The assembly material is given as 'outlines'. They are not manuscripts for you to learn and repeat to the children word perfect. Everyone is different in their personality, their gifts and abilities, their background and experience of the Christian faith. Bring your own individuality and creativity to the ideas in this book. Tell stories in your own way, work out your own illustrations, relate to the children in a way that you are comfortable with. Feel free to use and remodel this material – make it your own.

• Prepare the assembly content carefully:
  • memorise the outline;
  • work out, memorise and rehearse story-telling, games, activities, using an OHP etc;
  • think ahead to how you will integrate any audience participation easily and smoothly into your presentation;
  • think about any practical arrangements you need to make in the assembly room before the children come in or during the assembly. What do you need to do? How will you do it?
  • think in advance of a range of relevant illustrations and examples which you can use as necessary and appropriate;
  • if you are going to ask the children questions, or ask them for suggestions, anticipate how they might answer. This will help you to think about whether your question or request is phrased in the best way for this age group; and it will help

you to be prepared for any difficult or awkward contributions!

• if you want someone to play an instrument to accompany singing in the assembly, make sure that this is organised and that the musician has the relevant music.

Presentation

1 ATTENTION GRABBERS

Activities which interest, surprise, arouse curiosity, entertain, are all useful ways to start an assembly or to illustrate a point you wish to communicate to the children. However, don't let the 'attention grabber' take over. Remember, it is only the means to an end. You want the children to go away from the assembly remembering something about God or Jesus and their relationship with him, even if it is your attempts at juggling that they talk about at break-time (see 21 *I can't!* on page 82)!

2 STORYTELLING

Most of the stories used in this material are Bible stories. Sometimes they are given in outline and there are usually suggestions about the points which need to be emphasised. You will need to acquaint yourself thoroughly with the Bible story and devise your own way of telling it. Occasionally, it is suggested that you read a story straight from a modern version of the Bible, (eg the *Good News Bible* or the *International Children's Bible**).

Some points to remember:

• Stories, unless suggested otherwise, are usually best told from memory.

• Look at the children whilst you are telling the story or look away deliberately at specific points to create an effect, (eg 'They looked up ...' – you look up!).

• Be dramatic in the way you tell the story:

• use the emotions of the story (fear, excitement, happiness, humour, sadness, curiosity, suspense),

• use your body and voice to express the above;

• enter into the character roles in the story (see 2 *The Lost Sheep*, page 24).

• Make use of any opportunities for humour in the story.

• Help the children to feel the relevance of the story by adding in contemporary details (eg 'They were very hungry, but there wasn't a McDonald's nearby ...').

If you are using pictures or flash cards to help you tell the story, make sure all the children can see them and that any writing is large enough for everyone to see.

The contributors to this book have used a variety of methods of storytelling. You could apply some of these methods to your own assembly ideas:

a) Drama

• Ask some volunteers to act out the story as you tell it using a few props or items of clothing to suggest their roles, (eg 13 *Do what it says* on page 58).

• Take on the role of one of the characters in the story and tell it from that character's point of view.

• A stereo drama: two groups of children act out the story at the same time, as you tell it.

• Involve the whole audience by treating them as if they were part of the story, (eg 30 *Loaves and fishes*, on page 108, where all the children become the crowd at the feeding of the five thousand).

b) Props

• Use object or word clues which help move the story on. These can be hidden in advance and then discovered by volunteers during the telling of the story (eg 40 *Breakfast on the beach*, page 136 and 19 *Secrets*, page 74).

• Show object clues to keep the children guessing, and to help you tell the story, (eg 17 *God's got plans for you*, page 67).

• Use jointed pieces of brightly-coloured card, fixed together with paper fasteners to make the shapes of different objects referred to in the story. For more about this see 27 *Mistakes* on page 98.

c) Audience participation

Several of the outlines require the children to join in with various responses and sound effects, (eg 'Aah' and 'Eh?' in 27 *Mistakes* on page 98). Lots of Bible stories lend themselves to this kind of audience involvement. You can prompt the children's response with a catchphrase, (eg 'Whenever you hear me say this, you must say ...'), or with a flash card or large sign which is held up at the appropriate moment. The children will enjoy it and this method keeps them alert and attentive. There is more about audience participation below in point 3.

d) Pictures

• A story roll. This involves drawing large, simple pictures which illustrate the story on a roll of paper, (eg the back of an old roll of wallpaper, newsprint or lining paper). As you tell the story, unroll the pictures at the relevant moments.

• Draw simple illustrations on OHP acetates. If you are proficient at using an OHP, you could draw pictures which can be overlaid as you tell the story.

3   AUDIENCE PARTICIPATION

a) Volunteers

•   Many of the outlines suggest using volunteers. Think carefully during your preparation for the assembly about how their participation will work:

    • Where will you want your volunteers to stand?

    • Think about how you will keep your directions simple and easy for the children to follow.

•   Be careful not to embarrass a volunteer.

•   Don't leave your volunteers feeling stranded. Tell them when to go and sit down, when to give their props back, etc. Thank them for their help.

•   Even though your volunteers may be self-selecting (or excluding), remember that many children of this age will want to please you. They will put their hands up if they think you are asking them to! So, be sensitive to the personality and feelings of your volunteers. Enable them to opt out with dignity if you can see that they are uncomfortable with whatever you are asking them to do.

Some of the activities presume that your volunteer will have an extrovert personality, (eg the custard pie: 11 *Take your pick*, on page 53). Try to assess your volunteers and pick children who look as if they won't be upset by what you are going to ask them to do.

• Be very careful about the physical safety of the children.

If the assembly involves asking children to eat something, be aware of food allergies (to wheat, dairy produce, nuts, food colouring etc). Check with the school and with your volunteers.

• Be careful that you don't concentrate on your volunteers and their activities at the expense of the rest of the audience. Is it sufficiently interesting to keep the other children involved? Are they likely to get bored?

b) Whole audience participation

Whole audience participation helps to keep the children alert and attentive, waiting for the moment when they have to do or say something. It means everyone is involved and encourages a sense of 'ownership' of the assembly by the children.

• Make sure your instructions to the children are clear, so that they know what they are meant to do, when they are meant to do it and when they are meant to stop.

• Some outlines involve the children in making sound effects or various responses. Remember, if one hundred children are making a lot of noise together, they won't hear your one voice asking them to be quiet! Think in advance how you will establish quiet again. For example:

• Use flash cards which tell the children what to do or say. Include one which says, 'Quiet' or 'Stop'.

• Use a physical gesture as a pre-arranged signal that everyone needs to be quiet ('When I put my thumbs up/down/arms up ...' etc).

• Audience participation ends with a quiet sound, so that your voice can be heard.

c) Asking for children's suggestions and ideas

• The children will probably be very willing to contribute answers and ideas if you ask them. Sometimes these will be relevant, sometimes not! Anticipate what the children's contributions might be and think about how you will handle them. How will you use their ideas to lead you on to the next point you are aiming for?

• Keep the time short when you are asking for contributions from the children. Remember that while you listen to one child, the rest of the audience may not be feeling very involved.

• It's important that the children feel their ideas have been received in some way and are valued. To do this, you could:

  • write the children's suggestions onto an acetate and display them on an OHP;
  • write their ideas inside a relevant shape, (eg qualities of a hero inside a 'Superman' shape. See 31 *Heroes*, on page 111). This could be drawn on a large piece of card or onto an acetate for display on an OHP;
  • talk about their ideas briefly.

4 USING ILLUSTRATIONS

• Using illustrations, examples and anecdotes helps to keep the children's interest in what you are saying, and helps them to understand the points you wish to communicate.

• Make sure they are appropriate and relevant to the age group, and to the point you are trying to make.

• Children will enjoy personal anecdotes – you could use examples from your childhood. But don't be self-indulgent.

• Draw examples and illustrations from the children's world: local places, the pop groups they like, the football team most of them support, the TV programmes they watch, current fashions (clothes, food, games etc).

• Use humour.

Time of quiet

• The title of this section is a reminder that 'a prayer' does not have to be spoken aloud by the leader at this point.

• Children's lives are very busy and noisy. Perhaps a couple of minutes' silence, here, is all the quiet they will have during the day and is valuable in itself.

• Silence gives the children the opportunity for reflection on what they have heard and, hopefully, it will begin to help them learn the value of including times of stillness and quiet in their lives. Suggestions are given in the outlines as to what the children are expected to do with the silence.

• When a prayer is suggested in an outline, it is important that the children are given the option of joining in. Explain that the word, 'amen' is a way of saying you agree with the prayer. They might prefer to reflect on what has been said, rather than pray. You don't want the children to say things they don't mean or which aren't true for them. It's also important to remember that children from a variety of religious backgrounds will be present.

Song suggestions

Most primary schools do include singing in their assembly, but it is not essential for you to do so. You may feel that there isn't anything which fits your assembly very well or perhaps your assembly coincides with the weekly hymn practice.

Be sensitive to the ethos of the school and what the children are used to if you do decide to include singing. Some schools will be happy to tackle a new song, others will be more comfortable with what is familiar. Many primary schools have *Come and Praise 1 and 2*, BBC Books (see resource section on page 144 for details). The teacher responsible for music in the school will probably know the music from these books and may be happy to play for you. Check in advance what the children are used to and what the staff are comfortable with.

If you do decide to teach the children a song, you don't need to be a great singer/performer. The important thing is that you can sing in tune and keep to the correct time. If you can't play an instrument yourself, ask someone else to do it for you. Teach a song in the following way:

• sing the song through to the children yourself

• sing line 1 and ask the children to repeat it after you
• sing line 2 and ask the children to repeat it after you
• sing lines 1 and 2 together and ask the children to repeat the two lines
• sing line 3 ... and so on until the whole song has been learnt.

Song suggestions are included for each assembly, but they are not essential for an idea to work. Even though several suggestions are made for some of the outlines, no more than one song should be included in an assembly. It is up to you to decide at which point you wish to include singing, but often a song can make a natural conclusion for an assembly. Suggestions of song books which include material suitable for this age group are given in the resources list at the end of this book on page 144.

All the outlines in this book have been 'tried and tested'. Whatever your experience, background or role in school, we hope you will enjoy using this material, and that it will help you to share God – and his son, Jesus – with the children you meet in schools.

EVERYONE MATTERS

You're special

1 HOW MUCH ARE YOU WORTH?

Aim: To show that everyone is valuable to God.

Bible base: Matthew 6:26-30 – the lilies of the field.

You will need:

- A collection of objects, most of which are valuable in money terms. Include a few which are valuable to you because of the person they remind you of, or because of the memories they hold etc;
- Pictures of (or the actual items): a bar of soap, a nail, a cup of tea, some matches, a packet of *Epsom* salts (or equivalent), a tub of flea powder, a bucket of water.

Presentation

Introduction
1 Show the children your collection of valuable objects. Explain that all the things are very valuable to you. Ask the children which item they think is the most valuable.
2 Explain that the earrings (for example) are worth the most money, but the photo (for example) is the most valuable to you. Explain why.

What are you worth?
1 Comment that you've been thinking about objects, but how much are people worth? How valuable are we?
2 This is roughly what each adult human being is made up of. Show the pictures or items and talk briefly about each in turn:
- enough fat to make seven bars of soap

- enough iron to make one nail
- enough sugar for seven cups of tea (if you have sugar in your tea!)
- enough phosphorus to make about 2,200 matches
- enough magnesium for a dose of salts
- enough sulphur to rid one dog of fleas
- enough water to fill six buckets

Tell the children that if all these ingredients were sold, you would get less than ten pounds for them.

3 Talk about kidnapping. Even though the things which make up our bodies aren't *very* valuable, yet as people we are very valuable. Ask the children:

What would your mum and dad do if you were kidnapped? (... I expect they'd give anything to get you back!)

4 Talk about how, in spite of that, we sometimes don't feel very valuable. Ask the children to listen to what Jesus said about how much we are worth.

What the Bible says

1 Read some of Jesus' words from Matthew 6:26-30.

2 Tell the children that the Bible also says that God values us so much that he gave up the life of his son Jesus for us – as a sort of ransom (link with kidnapping) – so that we could be friends with him.

Conclusion

1 Comment that we look after valuable objects, so how much more should we care for people.

2 Ask the children:

How can we do this?

(Suggestions might include: being a friend to someone who is often left out; being especially kind to someone who is sad or hurt; being pleased for someone who passes an exam etc.)

3 Conclude by saying that all of us are special to God and we need to take care of each other.

Song suggestions

- Nobody's a nobody, 93, *The Big Book of Spring Harvest Kids Praise*
- You can weigh an elephant's auntie, 501, *Junior Praise 2*
- There is no one else like you, 476, *Junior Praise 2*

2 THE LOST SHEEP

Aim: To show that each one of us is special to God and he cares about us.

Bible base: Luke 15:1-7 – the lost sheep.

You will need:

- Use of an OHP
- 4 acetates, prepared as illustrated
- Large cuddly toy lamb

Preparation

- Copy or photocopy sheep drawings on to OHP acetates (see pages 25-28).
- Rehearse your telling of the story of the lost sheep along the lines suggested below.
- Familiarise yourself in advance with the layout of the hall where the assembly will take place.
- Hide 'Charlie' – the lost lamb – somewhere in the hall before the children come in.

Presentation

Introduction

1 Ask the children if any of them have ever been lost. Allow one or two to tell their stories.

2 Tell the children, briefly, about a time when you were lost. Use humour and a situation which the children can identify with.

3 Then give the example of starting at a new school (particularly useful for an assembly in September or October). It's easy to get lost (eg trying to find your way to the library and ending up in the girls'/boys' toilets). You need someone who can show you round, someone you can trust ... someone a bit like a shepherd who takes care of his sheep ...

Tell the story

Note: The storyteller needs to be ready to enter into the role of the shepherd, to help the children participate in the story and to make use of the opportunities for humour.

1 Explain that in Jesus' time there were lots of shepherds. The shepherd took his responsibility to look after the sheep very seriously. He would know them all individually (display **OHP 1**). At the end of the day, he would call his sheep and make sure they were all there before shutting them in the sheepfold for the night.

2 Tell the children that one day Jesus told a story about some sheep – and one that got away (display **OHP 2**).

3 Take on the role of the shepherd as you tell the story. Point to different children in the assembly as if they were the sheep. Pretend you are checking they are all there, 'Fred, Billy, Michelle ...' etc. Then say, 'BUT WHERE IS CHARLIE?!'

4 Explain that 'Charlie' was missing. The shepherd had got a choice: either he could go looking for Charlie, or he could say to himself, 'I've got loads of other sheep, I don't care about Charlie. I'm going home for a cup of tea and a bit of a rest while I watch *Neighbours* !'

5 Ask the children:
What do you think he did?

6 Agree with the children that, yes, he went off looking for Charlie. Taking on the role of the shepherd again, explain that he looked everywhere ... 'under the piano' ... 'behind the curtains' ... etc. (Use whatever the layout and contents of the hall suggest.)

7 Still in the role of the shepherd, explain that he went up to people he met (approach different children) and asked them, 'Excuse me, have you seen Charlie?' Encourage the children you approach to answer, 'yes' or 'no'.

8 Explain that by now the shepherd was tired and hungry, but he carried on – because he cared about Charlie so much. Eventually, he found him (discover Charlie wherever you hid him before the assembly). Be excited ('YEAH'), and throw Charlie on your shoulders! (Display **OHP 3**.)

9 Tell the children that the shepherd held a party with all his friends because he had found his lost sheep. The shepherd cared about all his sheep. Each one was special.

Application
Explain that the Bible says we are a bit like Charlie the sheep who got lost (ie we go off and do our own thing, make mistakes etc). Jesus is like the caring shepherd who comes and rescues us (display **OHP 4**). When we get ourselves in a mess by doing what's wrong, Jesus wants to help us make things right and to be able to live his way.

Conclusion
Conclude by telling the children that each one of us is valued by God, important and special. And even when we get lost sometimes (give examples), we're still special to God.

Song suggestions

- There is no one else like you, 476, *Junior Praise 2*
- Once upon a time, 443, *Junior Praise 2*

3 DON'T FORGET YOUR TOOTH BRUSH!

Aim: To show that although we're all different, we're all special to God in some way.

You will need:

- Various brushes: toothbrush, nail brush, pastry brush, hair-brush, make-up brush, paint brush, broom, brush (dustpan), toilet brush etc
- Tube of toothpaste

Presentation

1 Pretend that you got up late and had a real rush to get to school in time for the assembly. You had no time to brush your teeth. Ask the children if they mind you doing it now.

2 Take out a toilet brush (clean!). Put some toothpaste on it. Pretend you're going to brush your teeth. Act as though you're surprised if the children laugh. Ask them if it is the right brush.

3 Then show them various brushes, asking if each would do for brushing your teeth. Ask volunteers to come to the front and hold the brushes up for everyone to see as you discard them.

4 When you have shown the children several brushes, refer to each, explaining how they are specially made for the job they have to do (eg long handle for the loo etc).

Application

Point out to the children that in a similar way, God has made us all different. We are good at different things (eg long legs for running, a beautiful singing voice, being a good friend). And we're all special to him.

Time of quiet

1 In a short time of quiet, ask the children:
What's special about you?
What's special about your friends?
2 You could end with a prayer thanking God that each of the children is special and different and each can do different things well.

Song suggestions

- A naggy mum, 302, *Junior Praise 2*
- God knows me, 15, *Come and Praise 1*

—————— *Living with others* ——————

4 THE UNTOUCHABLES

Aim: To teach that God wants us to care for others, whatever they are like.

Bible base: Luke 5:12-14 – the man with leprosy.

You will need:

- Substances for 'feeling' game, concealed in appropriate containers, for example: flour, tomato sauce, jelly, shaving foam, raw egg.
- Blindfolds for 'feeling' game volunteers.
- A damp cloth and towel for children to clean up their hands after the game.
- Labels for each substance. The words should be written in large, clear letters so that they can be seen by all the children in the assembly.

Presentation

Feeling game

1 Ask for several volunteers to come to the front. Explain that you are going to ask each of them in turn to feel different substances concealed in containers. Put a blindfold on each of the volunteers. Each of them has to try and guess what they are feeling.

2 As each volunteer is doing this, show the rest of the children (but not the volunteers) the label which says what the mystery substance is.

3 Repeat this several times with different substances.

Talk about

1 Ask the children for suggestions of what they would find revolting to touch (risky, but worth doing!).

2 Explain that in Jesus' time, if you had leprosy (briefly explain what it is) no one would dream of touching you. They would have had the same kind of reaction to touching someone with leprosy, as you have to the things you find revolting. But Jesus was different ...

Tell the story

Read the story from Luke 5:12-14 straight from the Bible (*Good News Bible* or other modern version). You could ask for some volunteers to act out the story as you read it. A stereo drama can work well. This is where two groups act out the story at the same time, one group on either side of the 'stage' area.

Conclusion

1 Ask the children how they think the man with leprosy (or a 'dreaded skin disease') felt before Jesus had healed him, when others wouldn't come near him because of his illness. (Suggestions might include: lonely, ugly, unloved etc.)

2 Make the point that Jesus wasn't afraid of touching the man with the dreaded disease, and he wasn't scared of what others thought of him for doing it.

3 Comment that whilst none of them have got leprosy, maybe there are other things which sometimes make them feel like the odd one out. Tell the children to remember:

God loves them;

God wants them to care for others – especially those who often seem to be left out – whatever they're like, and whatever others think of them for doing it.

Song suggestions

- When I needed a neighbour, 275, *Junior Praise 1* and 65, *Come and Praise 1*
- Cross over the road, 498, *Junior Praise 1* and 70, *Come and Praise 1*

5 DO WHAT'S RIGHT

Aim: To help the children understand that when others tempt them to do something wrong, God can help them be strong enough to say, 'no'.

Bible base: Genesis 2:8–3:23 – the temptation of Eve and Adam.

You will need:

• Paper and pens for game participants

Preparation

• Prepare a quiz which illustrates the variety and beauty of nature (eg 'Name three yellow flowers', 'Name two animals with spots'). Devise a simple scoring system.
• Prepare questions for 'Choices' (see examples below), a game based on the *Scruples* game idea.

Presentation

Introduction
1 Ask for six to eight volunteers to make two teams. Play a simple quiz game about nature.
2 Tell the children that all these beautiful things remind you of the time when God planted a garden ...

Tell the story
1 Tell the story of creation and the temptation of Eve and Adam (see Genesis 2-3). Emphasise how the snake persuaded Eve to disobey God, and Eve persuaded Adam.
2 Comment that it's good to have friends – Adam would have been lonely in the garden without Eve. But sometimes our friends try to persuade us to do things which are wrong. Even

though we know they are wrong, we do them because we don't want to fall out with our friends.

Choices
1 Ask for seven volunteers to play 'Choices'.
2 Ask each of them one of the following questions (or similar):
a) If you had just got a new sweatshirt and then your friend said that the colour made them feel sick, would you wear it?
b) If your friends were playing a mean trick on someone you didn't like, would you join in?
c) If you weren't allowed to watch a TV programme that all your friends were watching regularly, would you argue with your mum?
d) If your friend was stuck with his spelling test, would you help him by showing him your answers?
e) If there was someone in your class who everyone said was 'stupid', would you make friends with them?
f) If you had promised to visit an old lady who was lonely and then your friend invited you round to play, would you still visit the old lady?
g) If your friend was in big trouble with the head teacher, would you tell a lie to get them off?
3 Ask your volunteers to write down a 'yes' or 'no' answer. They must keep their answers hidden from the audience. After each question, ask the rest of the children to vote on whether they think the person said, 'yes' or 'no'. Then ask the child to show their answer.

Conclusion
Conclude by saying that it can be hard to do what's right – and to say, 'no' when others want us to do what's wrong or when we are tempted to make the wrong choice. God wants to help us to be strong enough to do what is good and right.

Time of quiet

Invite the children to join in the following prayer by saying, 'amen' at the end if they would like to:

'Lord God, thank you for our friends. But sometimes our friends try to persuade us to do things and we don't know whether they are right or wrong. Please help us to be wise enough to know what's right and brave enough to do it. Amen.'

Song suggestions

- It's not very nice, 401, *Junior Praise 2*
- Do what you know is right, 12, *The Big Book of Spring Harvest Kids Praise*

Note: See also 38 *Give me strength!* on page 130.

6 WE NEED EACH OTHER

Aim: To show that God made each of us special and different – and we need each other.

Bible base: 1 Corinthians 12:14-21 – one body, many parts.

You will need:

- A soccer shirt (if possible use the colours of a team which you know will be popular with the children)
- A completed jigsaw with one piece missing, on a black back ground (optional)

Preparation

- Work out the body parts you will call out for the game (see below).

Presentation

The body game
1 Ask for eight volunteers. Divide them into two teams of four.
2 Explain that you are going to call out a number of body parts (eg two hands, two knees and two feet). Each team must organise itself so that only those parts are in contact with the ground. Team members can help one another and talk to each other. It's a race between the two teams.
3 Do this a few times, varying the body parts you call out. NB think carefully in advance about the groups of body parts you call out. Make sure it is actually possible for teams of four to do what you are asking them.

Talk about
1 When the game is finished, ask the children what qualities and skills were needed for the two teams to succeed (eg balance, communication, co-operation, decision-making etc).
2 Make the point that it was impossible to do the task successfully alone. The teams needed all their members to co-operate and contribute.

The soccer shirt
1 Ask for a volunteer to try on the soccer shirt.
2 Talk about how, in a soccer team, the individual players have different skills (goalkeeper, defender, midfield and forward players), yet they are all necessary for the team to succeed. Comment that, for example, a team made up of eleven 'Ryan Giggs' (or other current well-known player) might score loads of goals, but would be useless at defending etc. Emphasise again that everyone has to contribute their different gifts and abilities, if the whole team is to function well.

Talk about
1 Explain to the children that God has given each of them different gifts and abilities. They might not be great soccer players or able to sing like the band, Take That (or other current

example), but maybe they are good at listening or being a friend.
2 Explain that we need to try to do our best at everything, but we never need to feel jealous of anyone else. God has made us all different. We're all important and we all need each other.
3 Show the children the jigsaw puzzle (optional). Talk about the missing piece. Comment that even though the piece by itself doesn't seem very important, without it the jigsaw isn't complete. It's the same with us – we've all got a part to play.
4 Read 1 Corinthians 12:14-21 from the *Good News Bible* or another contemporary version. Explain that God has made each of us special, each of us unique.

Time of quiet

If appropriate you could conclude with a prayer like the following one:

> *'Father God, thank you that you have made each one of us special and different. Help us to use our different gifts to the best of our ability and to appreciate what others can do, as we live and work and learn together. Amen.'*

Song suggestion

• There is no one else like you, 476, *Junior Praise 2*

7 THE CARPENTER'S TOOLS

Aim: To help children understand that God made us all different. We all have different abilities and we all need each other. To make the best of what God has given us, we need to ask him to use us.

You will need:

- A tool box (a real one or a big box labelled 'tool box' containing:
  - a big hammer
  - a saw
  - a large screw driver
  - an electric drill

(You could make extra large 'pretend' tools instead of the real thing. These would be safer for the children to handle and would save you any anxiety about damage to expensive tools.)

Preparation

- Make a 'pretend' tool box and tools, if you have decided not to use the real thing.
- Prepare your telling of the story from memory, along the lines of the one given below. Think carefully about how you will integrate the contributions of the children into the story.

Presentation

Introduction

1 Tell the children that they will need to use their imaginations for the story you are going to tell them. You are going to ask them to imagine that they are in a place where they shouldn't really be – a building site. Comment briefly about the dangers of building sites.

2 Explain that you will need some of them to help you tell the story.

The story

Tell the following story using volunteers to help you with sound effects or actions at the points indicated. As the volunteers join in, they should stand across the front of the 'stage' area.

1 Begin the story:

It must have been the lunch-break – or something like that

– because all the builders had gone. The half-finished build-ing was deserted and quiet for the first time since the builders had arrived that morning. Wood, nails, bricks and cement all lay around and in the middle of them all was the carpenter's bag of tools. He would soon be returning after his meal to continue working.

While everyone was away there was a quiet, slow stirring amongst the chisels and pliers in the bag. **Henry Hammer** was the first to peer over the top. He had a shiny head with a big stubby nose.

2 At this point ask a volunteer to come and hold the hammer. Tell them that every time you mention a nail being knocked in you want **Henry** to shout, *'Bang!'*

Continue telling the story:

'I can make this house all by myself,' **Henry** thought. He smiled a smug smile. 'I don't need help from either the carpenter or any of the other tools. Where shall I start?' He looked around. A pile of floorboards lay nearby which needed to be nailed down. So he started fastening the boards to the floor with long sharp nails. He hit the nails in (*'Bang, bang!'*). **Henry** was so busy he didn't notice **Cynthia Saw** edge out of the bag, her teeth glinting at the thought of cutting wood.

3 Ask for another volunteer to hold the saw. Explain that every time **Cynthia Saw** cuts wood, you need to hear a, *'Zchee-schaw'* noise.

Continue the story:

Cynthia heard **Henry** all right. 'Jolly good luck to him,' thought **Cynthia**. 'I hope he's happy making all that noise – but I'm not going to help him. Why should I?' She looked around the half-finished building. 'I think I'll cut some wood for the staircase,' she thought. As soon as she got to the wood she started to cut (*'Zchee-schaw, Zchee-schaw'*). And **Henry** hammered (*'Bang, bang!'*) the nails in. **Sydney Screwdriver** was the next to appear.

4 Ask for another volunteer to hold the screwdriver. Explain that there is no noise for this tool. But every time **Sydney** is mentioned the *volunteer has to turn right round.*

Continue the story:

> **Sydney** looked at the other two tools. 'I don't need their help. They're so rough. I can build this place all by myself. What shall I do?'
>
> He looked around and noticed that the kitchen needed some shelving. 'I could do that – almost with my eyes shut. I'm so clever,' he thought.
>
> **Sydney** started twisting round (*volunteer turns round*). He put the brackets on, while **Cynthia** cut the wood ('*Zchee-schaw, zchee-schaw*'), and **Henry** hammered ('*Bang, bang!*') the nails in.
>
> By the time **Desmond Drill** appeared the place was a hive of activity. He was big, shiny and ... electric. Because he was an electric drill **Desmond** knew he was the most powerful tool and that, he believed, made him superior to everyone. He didn't think anyone could teach him anything. He looked at **Henry** and **Cynthia** and **Sydney** all working and thought how pathetic they were. He was much more interesting and strong and powerful.

5 Ask for another volunteer to hold the electric drill. Ask the children what noise an electric drill makes. They will probably make suggestions like, '*Whizz*'. Explain that this electric drill says, '*Black and Decker, Black and Decker*'!

Continue with the story:

> I could build this place by myself, **Desmond** thought. He looked around the site and noticed some cupboards needed putting up.
>
> **Desmond** started to drill the holes in the wall ('*Black and Decker, Black and Decker*'), while **Sydney** twisted (*volunteer turns round*), and **Cynthia** cut ('*Zchee-schaw, zchee-schaw*'), and **Henry** hammered ('*Bang, bang!*').
>
> After a little while, all the work stopped. It was quiet again. You see **Henry** had hammered in all the floorboards and

now needed **Cynthia** to cut some more. **Cynthia** had cut all the wood for the stairs and now needed Sydney to screw it together. **Sydney** had screwed in all the shelving and now needed **Desmond** to drill some more holes. **Desmond** had drilled all the holes for the cupboards and now needed **Sydney** to screw them in. It was at this point the tools made their first discovery: to build the best house possible they needed each other.

6 At this point make the first application of the story: each of us has different gifts and abilities. Some people are brilliant at maths or drama or football or English, but none of us can build a better world on our own. We need each other. We need to work together.

Continue telling the story:

So the four tools decided to cooperate.
'What shall we build first?' asked **Henry.**
'Something big!' shouted **Desmond**.
'With screws in,' **Sydney** added.
It was **Cynthia** who suggested a window frame – and they all agreed.

Cynthia was eager to cut the wood (*'Zchee-schaw, zchee-schaw'*), but the saw's teeth left it very rough and splintery. **Desmond** offered to help. He fitted a sanding disc on his nose and soon smoothed down all the splinters (*'Black and Decker, Black and Decker'*). He wanted to impress everyone but unfortunately he was too enthusiastic and he sanded too much off. Now the wood was too short.

'Never mind,' said **Sydney**, 'I'll put a screw in it, to hold it.' He twisted and twisted (*volunteer turns round*) and twisted, but the wood was very hard. 'I think we've chosen the wrong wood,' he sighed. 'I can't drive it in properly.'

'You're just a screw-turner,' said **Henry**, laughing rudely. 'I'm a real screw-driver.' He gave the screw the biggest bash he had ever given to anything (*'BANG!'*) and the window frame split from one end almost to the other. It was then that the tools made their second discovery.

7 At this point take the tools from the volunteers and send them back to their places.

Continue the story:

All along, the tools had ignored the carpenter, tried to use their own ideas and talents without him, and now the new building looked more like a demolition site. From now on, they would let the carpenter use them in whatever way he wanted.

Application

1 Tell the children that Jesus is sometimes called the carpenter from Nazareth (because he helped his father Joseph in his workshop).

2 Explain that Christians believe that God – like the carpenter – is the person who knows the best way of using our skills and abilities. So, if we want to build the best life possible and the best world possible, we need to ask 'the carpenter' (Jesus) to use us in whatever way he wants.

Time of quiet

Invite the children – if they would like – to join in the following prayer by saying, 'amen' at the end:

'Thank you, God, for all the different gifts and abilities you have given each of us. Please help us not to show off, but to use our talents for the good of others. Amen.'

Song suggestion

- The best gift, 59, *Come and Praise 1*

8 RULES FOR LIFE

Aim: To show that we need rules to help us live with each other.

You will need:

- An assistant
- A 'custard pie' (shaving foam on a paper plate – check it won't sting eyes)
- A blindfold
- Headphones

Preparation

Practise the Yes/no game (see 11 *Take your pick* on page 53, for the rules) with your assistant. They must be able to play the game without being caught out.

Presentation

The Yes/no game

1 Play the Yes/no game with your assistant. This involves asking a series of simple questions to which the obvious answers are 'yes' or 'no' (eg 'Are you female?' 'Is London the capital of England?' 'Does two add three to make four?'). But the person being asked the questions mustn't say 'yes' or 'no'. Tell the children that if your assistant makes a mistake he will get the 'custard pie'. Your assistant should not make any mistakes!

2 After a while, say to the children that this is getting boring, so you will change the rules.

3 Blindfold your assistant and give them a set of headphones and a *Walkman* to put on (assistant could hum along to imaginary music). Then, once your assistant apparently can't hear

what you are saying, discuss with the children possible rule changes to the game. Suggestions might include: the assistant gets the 'custard pie' if they *don't* answer 'yes' or 'no'; they should answer 'yes' to every question etc.

4 Take the blindfold and headphones off your assistant and play the game again – with the 'new' rules. That is, whatever answer your assistant gives to the questions, they get the 'custard pie'! (Make sure that your assistant is prepared!)

Application

1 Comment to the children that we need to know the rules or we can't play the game.

2 Explain that Christians believe God has given us rules for life, in the Bible. Ask the children for some examples (eg don't lie, don't steal, be generous). Talk briefly about how these make sense.

3 Explain that not only has God given us rules for living, he wants to help us keep them. That's why we pray. If we do break them, then he will forgive us and help us to learn from our mistakes.

Time of quiet

1 Tell the children that the Lord's Prayer is really about asking God to help us live his way. Pick out some of the lines which are particularly relevant to what you have been talking about.

2 Invite the children to join with you, if they would like to, in saying the Lord's Prayer. (Check with the teacher beforehand if the children know this prayer. You may wish to have the words written on a large piece of card or on an OHP acetate to help them.)

Song suggestions

- The baked beans song, 390, *Junior Praise 2*
- God loves you so much, 349, *Junior Praise 2* and 28, *The Big Book of Spring Harvest Kids Praise*

Note: See also 13 *Do what it says,* on page 58; 29 *Try it and see,* on page 104 and 37 *Recipe for ... pancakes!* on page 127. These assemblies also focus on the Bible.

GOD AND ME

9 GOD KNOWS HOW YOU FEEL

Aim: To help children understand that God knows and cares about how we are feeling.

Bible base: Psalm 139:1-6 – God knows everything about us.

You will need:
• Paper plates
• Felt-tip pens

Presentation

1 Tell the children that you are going to be thinking about feelings in this assembly.
2 Ask for five to seven volunteers who are good at drawing. Give them each a paper plate and felt-tips and ask each of them to draw one of the following: a face which is happy, sad, excited, angry, frightened etc. (If it is a small group assembly, you could ask all the children to do this, then pick some volunteers to show their 'faces'.)
3 Ask your volunteers to show their 'faces' in turn to the rest of the children. As they do so, ask them to say, 'I feel happy (sad, excited etc) when ...' and then give an example of what makes them feel like that. Ask your volunteers to sit down.
4 Explain to the children that sometimes, like the paper plate faces they have drawn, your feelings show on your face. Sometimes, though, no one else can tell how you are feeling inside – but God knows.
5 Tell the children that you are going to read them a poem written hundreds of years ago. It was written by a man called David who wrote lots of the poems or songs called Psalms in the Bible. Read from the *Good News Bible*, or other contemporary version, Psalm 139:1-6.
    Comment that, however David was feeling, he knew God understood him and was with him, ready to help him.

Time of quiet

Ask the children to think about how they are feeling now. Remind them that God knows and understands their feelings and will help them if they ask him.

Song suggestions

- My Lord is higher than a mountain, 170, *Junior Praise 1*
- From my knees to my nose, 342, *Junior Praise 2*

10 GETTING RID OF YOUR RUBBISH

Aim: God is willing to forgive the wrong in our lives.

Bible base: 1 John 1:9 – if we confess our sins to God, he will forgive us.

You will need:

- Washing-up bowl containing warm water, brush, cloth and tea towel
- A few dirty jars (eg jam jars, coffee jars etc)
- Newspapers which contain colour photos
- Scissors (with rounded ends)
- Some large potatoes
- A potato peeler
- A rubbish bag clearly labelled 'compost'
- Four pieces of card with the following written on them: 'GIV', 'ESS', 'FOR', 'ENE'

Preparation

- Before the assembly begins arrange three small tables at the front with the following props on them:
  - Table 1: washing-up bowl with water, brush, cloth, tea towel and the dirty jars
  - Table 2: newspapers and scissors
  - Table 3: potatoes, potato peeler and rubbish bag

Presentation

Introductory activity

1 Ask for three volunteers. Tell them you have a special job for each of them:
  - wash up your dirty jar
  - cut out the colour photos from the newspapers – you need them for something
  - peel the potatoes and put the peel in the rubbish bag for your compost bin

2 While your volunteers are working at their tasks, ask the rest of the children to think of a connection between the three activities. Hold up bits of 'rubbish' as clues (an empty, dirty jar, an old newspaper, potato peel). The three activities are all about recycling your rubbish.

Recycling your rubbish

1 While your volunteers are finishing their tasks, take a survey to find out who recycles glass, paper and compost.

2 Comment that recycling is one good way of getting rid of the rubbish we can see. Explain that humans also produce rubbish that we can't see or touch, for example: anger, hatred, rudeness, fighting. There are lots of bad things like this that people are capable of producing. Ask the children how we can get rid of these things:

Is there an 'anger bank'? Or a 'hatred recycling bin'?

No, there isn't! We can't 'recycle' the 'rubbish' that is in us or in other people. We simply need to get rid of it. Ask the children:

How can we do that?

Forgiveness

1 Ask for four volunteers to hold up the four pieces of card. Ask your volunteers to stand in a line across the front of the 'stage' area. Tell the children that when the letters are arranged correctly they will spell a very important word. Ask for a volunteer to rearrange the letters so that they spell the word you are looking for. (Answer: forgiveness.)

2 Explain to the children that the way we can get rid of rubbish like anger, hatred etc is through forgiveness. Give some examples that the children can relate to. For example, if someone hurts you – with a thump or unkind words – don't hold a grudge, don't try to get even. Forgive them. Tell them you'd still like to be friends. If you started the trouble, say you're sorry. (Maybe you have got a personal anecdote you could tell the children to illustrate the point.)

3 Comment that sometimes it is very hard to forgive. Tell the children that you know someone who will always forgive us, no matter how bad we've been. Ask the children if they can guess who you are talking about. Tell them that the Bible says, if we say sorry to God for the wrong things we have done – and mean it – he will forgive us completely (see 1 John 1:9). Emphasise God's great kindness in doing this for us. In other words, God does away with our rubbish by forgiving us and forgetting all about the wrong things we have done. Tell the children that we need to do the same for one another.

Time of quiet

- Tell the children that, if they would like to, they can join in with this prayer by saying, 'amen' at the end:
  'Dear Father God, thank you that you love us so much that you forgive us for all our 'rubbish' when we say sorry to you. Help us to forgive others too when they say or do things that hurt us. Amen.'
- *Alternatively,* you could remind the children of the line in the Lord's Prayer, 'Forgive us our sins as we forgive those who sin against us'. Make the link with what you have been talking about in the assembly. If the children are used to saying the Lord's Prayer in assembly, say it with them now.

Song suggestions

* I'm special, 106, *Junior Praise 1*
* Sorry Lord, 463, *Junior Praise 2*
* Everybody join in singing this song, 332, *Junior Praise 2*

Note: See also 23 *Forgiveness*, on page 89 and 27 *Mistakes*, on page 98. These assemblies also focus on the theme of forgiveness.

11 TAKE YOUR PICK

Aim: To show that everyone has choices to make about God which have consequences for our lives.

You will need:

* 3 large boxes which contain: a) a chocolate bar, b) a tin of spaghetti with a can opener, a bowl and spoon, c) a 'pie' made of shaving foam (check it won't sting eyes) on a paper plate
* 3 labels for the boxes: 1, 2, 3
* 3 large card keys (numbered)
* A toy microphone (optional)
* A wet cloth and a towel for cleaning up volunteers
* 4 flash cards with words as follows: a) ignore him, b) find out more about him, c) believe in him, d) follow him

Preparation

* Arrange the props for 'Take your pick' before the assembly begins.

- Prepare questions for volunteers to answer (see 8 *Rules for life* on page 45.)

Presentation

Introduction

1 Talk to the children about choices. Explain that our lives are full of them (what you will eat, wear, what secondary school you will go to etc). The choices we make have consequences for our lives.

2 Explain that you are going to play a game which shows that.

Yes/no game

1 Ask for three volunteers to play the Yes/no game. Explain that the winner will play 'Take your pick'.

2 If you like, you could use the toy microphone at this point to help establish your role of game show presenter.

3 The game is played as follows:

Ask each volunteer in turn a question which needs a 'yes' or 'no' answer.

- However, the contestant must not say, 'yes' or 'no', but find another way of answering.
- Whenever a contestant does say, 'yes' or 'no', ask them to sit down.
- Continue until there is one player left. They (the winner) are now entitled to play, 'Take your pick'.

Take your pick

Be ready to make use of all the opportunities for creating an atmosphere of suspense, of humour etc.

1 Tell the winner of the Yes/no game that they can choose one key to open one box. Explain that in one box there is a mystery prize that they will probably enjoy. In the other two there are things which they might *not* like the consequences of … They have to choose – and take the consequences!

2 Hold out the three 'keys' for the child to choose.

3 The child opens the chosen box – and then takes the consequences:

the bar of chocolate – theirs to take away and enjoy.

the tin of spaghetti – they must open it with your help (if necessary), put some in a bowl and eat it (cold) in front of all the other children.

the 'custard pie' (apply it to the side of the face; give child time to prepare).

4 Offer a damp cloth and towel if necessary and help your volunteer to clean up.

Talk about

1 Comment that life is full of choices big and small. Some don't matter too much. Others – like the job we do, or deciding whether to get married or not – will have very big consequences for our lives.

2 Explain that Christians believe we all have important choices to make about God. The choices we make about him have big consequences for our lives, too. The choices are (show relevant flash card as you talk about each of the following):

- ignore him
- find out more about him
- believe in him
- follow him

3 Talk briefly about these choices and especially the consequences for our lives of 'follow him'.

Time of quiet

- Ask the children to think about what choice they will make about God.
- Encourage them to ask God to help them choose to live his way – to follow him.

Song suggestion

- Put your hand in the hand, 206, *Junior Praise 1*

12 CHOOSE LIFE

Aim: To show that God offers everyone the gift of life. To receive it, we need to be ready to let go of other things which seem important to us.

Bible base: Matthew 19:16-30 – the rich young ruler.

You will need:

- Clothes to suggest rich man/woman
- 8-10 heavy 'money bags' (see Preparation below)
- A large shoe box, gift-wrapped (Christmas or birthday as appropriate). Tie a tag on the parcel on which is written clearly in large letters:
  'To the rich man. Free gift. Love, God.'

Preparation

- Make the 'money-bags' by wrapping up large stones securely in brown paper. Make a traditional money-bag shape by tying string round the paper to form a 'neck'. Write the pound sign in black felt-tip pen on each bag. Alternatively, you could use a water melon as the base for a money-bag, in which case, three or four 'money-bags' would be enough.
- Prepare gift-wrapped box and tag.

Presentation

1 Ask for a volunteer to play the part of a very rich person. Dress up your volunteer as appropriate. You could give the rich person a name (eg Lady Lots-of-lolly, Sir Magnus Moneybags etc).

2 Ask the children what they think might be on the birthday or Christmas present list of your rich person (eg a car, a bigger house, a yacht, a CD-ROM etc).

3 As each suggestion is made, say to the 'rich' person, 'I'm

sorry, I don't happen to have a yacht (car, house etc) with me, but here is some money to buy one.' Hand the volunteer a money-bag.

4 Continue like this with several suggestions until your volunteer is staggering under the weight and unable to hold any more 'money-bags'.

5 Ask for another volunteer to pick up the gift-wrapped parcel and read the words on the gift tag out to everyone.

6 Tell the children that as it's Sir Magnus Moneybags' (use whatever name you have chosen) birthday (or because it's Christmas), God has a present for the rich person, too. Ask the volunteer to give the parcel to the rich person.

7 Focus on the dilemma of the rich man. If he wants to accept God's gift, he must put the money-bags down. Ask your two volunteers to wait a moment.

8 Ask the rest of the children to shout their advice. Should the rich man: *Open the box or keep the money?*

9 Once the point is made, ask your volunteers to sit down.

Tell the story
1 Explain that Jesus told a story about a rich man who had to make a choice between what he wanted – his money or following Jesus.

2 Tell the story of the rich young ruler.

Conclusion
Explain that, although we may not be rich like the man in the story, we also have a choice: we can do what we want and keep God out; or we can accept God's gift of life, which means choosing to live his way and knowing that he is with us always.

Song suggestion

• When Jesus walked in Galilee, 25, *Come and Praise 1*

Note:
1. This assembly could be followed up with another, focusing on what is in the gift from God or it could be used near Christmas-time thinking about Jesus as the gift from God.
2. See also 24 *The price is right,* page 92. This assembly looks at friendship with Jesus as the treasure which is discovered inside the box.

13 DO WHAT IT SAYS

Aim: To show that it makes sense to do what the Bible says.

Bible base: Matthew 7:24-27 – the two builders.

You will need:

- 2 hats: a builder's hard hat if possible for the 'wise man' and a 'silly' hat (or a knotted handkerchief would do) for the 'foolish man'.
- A flash card (optional). On one side is written the word, 'Aha!' and on the other, the word, 'Er'.

Preparation
- Practise telling the story, using the two hats, the words 'Aha!' and 'Eer' and their accompanying gestures. Decide at which points the children will join in. For example:
  'Anyone who hears these words of mine (Aha!) and obeys them (Aha!) ...'
  'The rain poured down (Er), the rivers overflowed (Er) ...'

Presentation

Introduction

Talk to the children about houses: Who lives in what type? If any of them have watched a house being built, what is built first? etc.

Tell the story

1 Tell the children that you would like them to help you tell a story. You would like them to join in with you with the following words and gestures:

- 'Aha!' – said with a look of triumph and accompanied by a gesture of raising the index finger of one hand as though a good idea has occurred to you.
- 'Er' – said with a puzzled look and a gesture of holding your chin in a perplexed manner.

2 Demonstrate this and then give the children a practice.

3 Tell the story of the two house builders. Put on the two different hats at the appropriate moments. Provide as many opportunities as possible for the children to join in with, 'Aha!' and 'Er'. You could help them to join in by showing the flash card at the appropriate moments (optional).

Alternatively, you could ask two children to wear the hats and to mime the actions whilst you tell the story, and everyone else joins in with the words ('Aha!' and 'Er') and gestures.

Application

1 Explain to the children that Jesus told us that hearing and doing what the Bible says is to be like the wise man in the story. (You could put the builder's hat back on at this point.)

2 Ask the children for some examples of things that the Bible says we should do:

- respect your mum and dad (Exodus 20:12)
- don't steal (Exodus 20:15)
- don't criticise other people (Matthew 7:1)
- don't show off how good you are (Matthew 6:2) etc

Help them to see that those things make sense for us today. Help them to think about ways in which they could do what the

Bible says.

Song suggestions

- The baked beans song, 390, *Junior Praise 2* (Talk about the line which says, 'Don't put your Bible out of sight if you want to know what's right.')
- Don't build your house on the sandy land, 39, *Junior Praise 1*

Note: See also 8 *Rules for life*, on page 45; 29 *Try it and see*, on page 104 and 37 *Recipe for ... pancakes!* on page 127. These assemblies also focus on the Bible.

14 LISTENING

Aim: To help children think about listening to God.

Bible base: 1 Samuel 3 – Samuel hears God speaking to him.

Presentation

Introduction
Talk to the children about listening. Explain how we all need to listen. Give examples: traffic sounds when crossing the road, a warning shout, what our parents and teachers tell us. If we ignore these sounds we suffer the consequences.

Game
1 Ask for two volunteers. Explain that you are going to play a word association game. The two players must take it in turns to say a word to do with the given subject. The first one to hesitate or repeat a word that has already been said is out. That

player will be replaced by another volunteer for round two and so on until you have a winner.

2 Play four rounds as follows:
- round one – objects that make sounds at home (eg radio, clock, doorbell)
- round two – objects that make sounds on the way to school (eg cars, talking, trains)
- round three – objects that make sounds at school (eg computer, music, bell)
- round four – objects that make sounds on the farm (eg tractor, cows, chickens)

Think spot

1 Comment to the children that we are surrounded by noise all day long (eg TV, talking, music etc). Sometimes we don't really hear what other people say to us, even though we might look as though we're listening. Give an example which will be relevant to the children's everyday experience. The example might end, for example, with Mum saying, 'But I told you to ...' and child replying, 'I didn't hear you.'

2 Comment that we need to learn to be still, and to be able to concentrate, to listen properly to someone speaking to us. Then we can really hear what they are saying.

Tell the story

Tell the story of Samuel being spoken to by God (see 1 Samuel 3). Emphasise that the fourth time God spoke to him, Samuel at last sat still and listened – so he heard what God wanted to say to him.

Conclusion

1 Explain that Samuel had to learn to be quiet and listen to God.

2 We have to learn to listen to others speaking to us: parents, teachers, friends etc.

3 Explain that the Bible teaches that God wants to speak to us, too (eg to stop us being unkind to someone, telling us not to lie and to tell us that he loves us etc). In order to hear God speak-

ing we need – like Samuel – to be quiet and listen to him.

Time of quiet

1. Ask the children to think about how busy and noisy they are sometimes; then to think about how God spoke to Samuel.
2. Invite the children to listen to the following prayer, and if they agree, to join in by saying, 'amen' at the end:
Thank you, God, that you taught Samuel to stop, be quiet, and listen to you. Help me to listen to you also. Amen.'

Song suggestions

- Did you ever talk to God above?, 329, *Junior Praise 2*
- I listen and I listen, 60, *Come and Praise 1*

15 TALK TO GOD – HE'S LISTENING

Aim: To teach children that we can talk to God at any time, anywhere – and he is always listening.

Bible base: Philippians 4:6 – ask God for what you need with a thankful heart.

You will need:

- 4 pieces of card with the following words written clearly on them:
  - please
  - thank you
  - sorry
  - you're great!

Preparation

- In this assembly, you will be promising to answer the children's questions honestly. It's worth thinking in advance about the kind of questions they might ask – and how you will answer!
- In advance, find a volunteer – one of the children – to read Philippians 4:6 (from a modern translation) in the assembly.

Presentation

Introduction

1 Ask the children to imagine that you are a new pupil in their class who has just arrived. Ask the children:

How would you get to know me? (Listen to their suggestions.)

2 Comment that one way would be by asking you questions about yourself. Ask the children what questions they would like to ask you. Say that you promise to answer them truthfully. (Answer a few of their questions.)

3 Comment that if you were going to be friends, one way to start is by talking to each other. Tell the children that in this assembly you are thinking about one way in which we can be friends with God – by talking to him. Ask the children if they can tell you the special word we use when we mean talking to God. (Answer: prayer).

What the Bible says

1 Tell the children that you are going to find out what the Bible says about prayer. They need to listen very carefully to see if they can hear some of the things we can pray about.

2 Ask your reader to come to the front and read Philippians 4:6.

Talk about

1 Ask the children:

So, what sorts of things can we pray about?

2 Encourage the children to give actual examples of the kinds of things they might want to pray about. Philippians 4:6 empha-

sises 'asking' and 'thanking' prayers, so you may need to help the children think about the 'sorry' and 'you're great!' kind of prayers as well. As they make suggestions, use the four cards to show what kind of prayer it is. For example, if a child says we can pray for our families, talk about 'please' prayers, whilst holding up the relevant card.

Include the following categories:

'Thank you' prayers – the Bible teaches that God has given us everything we have, so we can thank him for all he's given us.

'Please' prayers – we can ask God for what we need or help for anything we are worried about. We shouldn't ask God for wrong things.

'Sorry' prayers – sometimes we do, say or think something that God doesn't like and that is wrong. We need to say sorry to God and to ask him to help us not to do it again.

'You're great!' prayers – The Bible teaches that God is the most important, most powerful, most wonderful person in the whole universe. It's good to tell him how great he is and to thank him that he wants to be our friend.

3 Ask the children:

When can we pray?

(Ask for suggestions, leading to the answer: any time.)

Where can we pray?

(Ask for suggestions, leading to the answer: anywhere.)

Conclusion

1 Recap what you have learnt about prayer.

2 Tell the children that now you want to tell them something very important. The Bible tells us that when we talk to God (pray), God listens – because he cares about us and wants to be our friend.

Time of quiet

1 Ask the children for suggestions of things they would like to say thank you to God for.

2 Conclude the assembly with some of these 'thank you' prayers.

Song suggestions

- Prayer is like a telephone, 448, *Junior Praise 2* and 101, *The Big Book of Spring Harvest Kids Praise*
- When the dark clouds, 494, *Junior Praise*

16 GOD MADE ME

Aim: To show that God made all things – including human beings – and he cares about us.

Bible base:
Genesis 1-2 – God made everything;
Matthew 6:25-30 – God cares about his creation.

You will need:

- A selection of items that someone has made. Choose things that will interest the children; for example: a pottery mug (or other piece of pottery), a completed Lego model, a painted picture, a model aeroplane/boat etc.
- An audio cassette of animal sounds and cassette player.
- An OHP, acetates and pens, or flip-chart and pens (optional).

Preparation

- Record short examples of animal sounds.

Presentation

What's the connection?
Show the children the items you have brought. Ask the children:

What's the connection between them?
(Answer: they have all been made by someone.)

Brainstorm
1 Ask the children how many different things they can think of that you might see or hear outside on a beautiful summer's day (eg trees, flowers, birds singing, butterflies etc).
2 Write the children's suggestions on the OHP or flip chart (optional).

Guess the sound
1 Play the audio cassette of animal sounds.
2 Ask the children to guess what is making each of the sounds.

Talk about
1 Comment to the children that there are many amazing and beautiful things in the world. But who made them? Explain that some people think they just somehow happened. Christians believe that they were all made/started by God.
2 Talk about who made us. Comment that there are different ideas about how human beings started. Explain that Christians believe, and the Bible says – even though we don't understand exactly how it all happened – that we were made by God.
3 Ask the children:
Who likes making Lego models?
What sort of things do you make with it?
How do you feel when you have just made a really good Lego model?
(Answers might be: proud, pleased, want to show it to others, want to take care of it.)
What might you do with it a few days later?
(Answers might be: smash it up, be bored with it, forget about it.)

Conclusion
1 Ask the children how they think God feels about what he has made – the world and especially, us. Tell the children that the Bible says God was very pleased with the world he had made. He's proud of us and cares about us very much. He

doesn't forget about us, get bored with us and he doesn't want us to get hurt.

2 Ask the children, next time they go outside on a beautiful day:

• to thank God for the world he has made.

• to remember that he has made each of them and cares about them.

Song suggestions

• He made the water wet, 359, *Junior Praise 2*
• God knows me, 15, *Come and Praise 1*
• He made me, 18, *Come and Praise 1*

Note: Early summer would be an especially good time to use this assembly outline.

17 GOD'S GOT PLANS FOR YOU

Aim: To show that God has a plan for our lives and that he can bring good out of the bad things that happen to us.

Bible base: Genesis 37, 39-41 – Joseph's story.

You will need:

• Clues for telling the story, to be used in this order:
  1 a brightly-coloured jacket or coat
  2 a toy camel and map
  3 cleaning equipment (eg washing-up gloves, mop and bucket etc)
  4 a pair of handcuffs (you can get toy ones)

5 a bread roll and a bunch of grapes
6 a 'Don't forget' sticker or label
7 party popper, streamers, party hat etc
- OHP acetate or large piece of thin card with drawing showing the highs and lows of Joseph's life (optional)

Preparation

- Memorise and rehearse telling the story of Joseph. Think carefully about how the children will participate and about the use of the 'clues'.
- Before the assembly begins, give each 'clue' to a different child. Ask them to look after their clue. Explain that the clues are to help you tell a story during the assembly. You will want them to bring their clue to the front to show everyone at the appropriate moment in the story.

Presentation

Introduction
Tell the children that you are going to tell them a story which you think they might know. Explain that they are going to see various 'clues' during the telling of the story, and you want them to tell you what happens next.

Tell the story
Call the children with the clues to the front in turn as you are telling the story of Joseph. Ask them to show their clues to the other children. Use the clues together with the children's help to tell the story. Fill in what they don't know.

CLUE 1 (the coat)
Ask the children:
Who knows who this Bible story might be about?
Why did Joseph have a special coat?
(Answer: he was his father's favourite.)
How did his brothers feel about this?

CLUE 2 (the camel and the map)
Ask the children:
What did Joseph's brothers do to him?

CLUE 3 (mop and bucket etc)
1 Ask the children:
What happened to Joseph once he was in Egypt?
2 Comment that the Bible says God was with him and made him a success. Use any opportunities for humour (eg Joseph must have been good at cleaning the loos!)

CLUE 4 (the handcuffs)
1 Ask the children:
Then what happened?
2 Stress that Joseph hadn't done anything wrong, but someone told lies about him. His master believed the lies and Joseph was thrown into prison.
3 Tell the children that the Bible says God was with him and made him successful at being a prisoner! The jailer noticed Joseph and gave him responsibility over the other prisoners.

CLUE 5 (a bread roll and bunch of grapes)
1 Ask the children:
Which two people come into the story next?
2 Talk about the baker and the wine-taster and their dreams.

CLUE 6 (the 'Don't forget' sticker)
1 Ask the children:
What did Joseph ask the wine-taster to do?
(Answer: not to forget him when he got his job back.)
2 Explain that two years went by and then ...

CLUE 7 (party popper etc)
1 Let off party popper, throw streamers (ask some of the children to help), put on the party hat.
2 Explain that although the Bible doesn't say, you expect Joseph celebrated when he was brought from prison to be second-in-command in the whole country!

Application

1 Tell the children that Joseph's life was a bit like a roller-coaster. Indicate the following pattern with exaggerated movements of your hand, commenting on the various highs and lows as you do so:

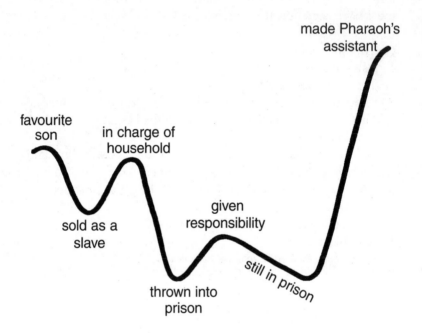

(Or this could be shown on an OHP acetate or large piece of card.)

2 Comment that God was with Joseph in the good times and in the bad times. And God brought good out of all the terrible things which happened to Joseph – both for Joseph, himself, and for many other people.

3 Explain that Christians believe that God has a plan for our lives. Things sometimes go wrong (in our families, illness etc), but God can bring good out of the bad things in our lives, if we let him.

Time of quiet

1 Ask the children if there is anything they are feeling sad about at the moment or finding difficult.

2 Remind them that God has a plan for their lives. He knows about the situation and is with them in it.

3 Invite the children to join with you in the following (or similar) prayer, if they'd like to, by saying, 'amen' at the end:

Thank you, God, that you have a plan for our lives. Thank you that you are with us in the good times and the bad times. We especially ask that you will be with and help anyone here who is going through a difficult time at the moment. Amen.'

Song suggestions

* If you climb, 388, *Junior Praise 2*
* The journey of life, 468, *Junior Praise 2* and 45, *Come and Praise 1*

18 HOW TO BE A FROG

Aim: To show that, with God in our lives, we can be what we're meant to be.

Bible base: John 3:1-8 – the story of Nicodemus.

You will need:

- Two identical brown paper bags – McDonald's 'takeaway' bags work well
- Two pictures – a butterfly and a frog
- Two pieces of paper and felt-tip pens or pencils

Preparation

- Glue the two paper bags together, so that they look like one bag. It should still be possible to open both bags separately.
- Place the pictures of the butterfly and the frog into one of the bags.

Caterpillar and tadpole to be placed in this side during assembly.

Place butterfly and frog in this side before assembly.

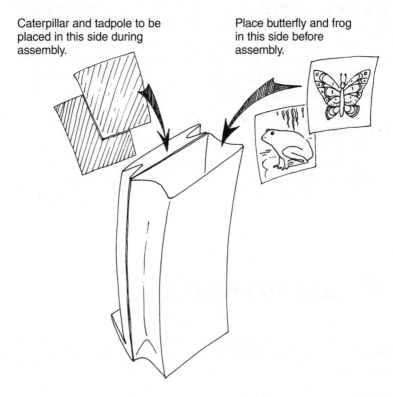

- Prepare your telling of the story using the paper bags and pictures as outlined below.

Presentation

Tell the story

1 Tell the story of Nicodemus to the point where Jesus tells him that, 'to see the kingdom of God' you need to be 'born again' (John 3:3). Explain any terms which might be difficult for the children as simply and briefly as possible, and in a way which is appropriate to the children and to the school.

2 At this point, ask the children if they can think of two living creatures which start off as one thing and then change to another. Help the children towards the answer:

caterpillars and tadpoles.

3 Ask for two volunteers to do drawings of a caterpillar and a tadpole.

4 Show the drawings to the rest of the children and then place them into the empty side of the 'bag'. As you put the bag down, turn it over, so that the side with the frog and the butterfly is uppermost.

5 Continue telling the story. Explain how Nicodemus found what Jesus said difficult to understand. Jesus told him that such a change was only possible with God (the Holy Spirit).

6 Pick up the 'bag'. Take out the pictures of the frog and the butterfly. Emphasise that the caterpillar and tadpole have changed into what they were meant to be.

Application

1 The best for us in life is to know God and to live his way.

2 Nicodemus was right – we can't do that by ourselves. It's impossible.

3 With God (the Holy Spirit) in our lives, it *is* possible – and we can be the best God meant us to be.

Time of quiet

1 In a short time of silence, remind the children that we can choose to live without God in our lives, or we can ask him to help us in our lives.

Ask the children:

So, do you want to stay a tadpole or would you rather be a frog?!

2 Invite the children to join in a prayer similar to this, if they would like to, by saying, 'amen' at the end:

'Father God, we can't live your way without your help. So please change us, so that we can be the best we can for you. Amen.'

Song suggestions

- When Jesus walked in Galilee, 25, *Come and Praise 1*
- Jesus, send me the helper, 409, *Junior Praise 2*

19 SECRETS

Aim: To show that God wants to be with us and help us to live our lives for him.

Bible base: The book of Esther.
    2:10,20 – Secret 1 (Esther's);
    2:21-23 – Secret 2 (Mordecai's);
    3:5-6 – Secret 3 (Haman's);
    4:15 – 5:8 – Secret 4 (Esther's);
    5:9-14 – Secret 5 (Haman's);
    6:1-11 – Secret 6 (the king's);
    7 – Secret 7 (Esther's).

You will need:

- Labels to hang on volunteers: Esther, Mordecai, Haman, the king
- 7 envelopes with 'Secret 1', 'Secret 2' etc, written on outside. Each envelope contains a 'secret' written clearly on a piece of paper

Preparation

- Before the assembly find out some 'secrets' about some of the children and teachers (pets, hobbies, parents' jobs, foot ball team supported etc). The people concerned should be surprised that you know their secret, but do not use anything which is likely to cause real embarrassment.
- Prepare the labels for the story characters.
- Write each secret clearly on a sheet of paper and place in its envelope. The secrets are:
    Secret 1 (Esther's) – I am Jewish.
    Secret 2 (Mordecai's) – I discovered a secret plot to ass-asinate the king.
    Secret 3 (Haman's) – I made a secret plan to kill Mordecai – and all the Jews.
    Secret 4 (Esther's) – I made a dangerous and secret plan to save my people from extermination.
    Secret 5 (Haman's) – I built some gallows – secretly – ready for Mordecai.
    Secret 6 (the king's) – I made a secret plan to reward Mordecai.
    Secret 7 (Esther's) – I have a secret plan: I am going to tell the king about Haman's secret plot.
- Read and learn the story of Esther thoroughly. The outline given below covers the main points, but it is not intended to be used as a manuscript. You need to prepare and memorise your own telling of the story and to work out how and when you will integrate the 'secrets' into your presentation.

Presentation

Introduction
Tell the children that the theme of the assembly is 'secrets'. Share some of the 'secrets' about pupils and teachers that you have discovered.

Tell the story
Note: The story is told by moving from 'secret' to 'secret'. You

could use the ones given above, or you could work out different 'secrets' from the story.

1 Ask for four volunteers to represent four of the characters in the story you are going to tell. Ask them to stand across the front of the 'stage' area.

2 Tell the children that you are going to tell them about a beautiful and brave woman called Esther. With great courage and daring she saved her people, the Jews, from extermination. Explain that it's a Bible story found in the Old Testament and happened at the time when the Jewish people had been captured and were living in exile in the Persian Empire.

3 Put the labels on your four volunteers, introducing their characters as you do so:

Esther – the heroine of the story;

Mordecai – Esther's good and wise cousin, who had brought her up and held a high position in the king's government;

Haman – the wicked Persian prime minister;

The king – the emperor of Persia, crazy about Esther, whom he made his queen.

4 Tell the children that it is a story full of secrets and that all will be revealed as they listen. Move from secret to secret. Use the outline below, asking the four volunteers to read out their 'secrets' to the rest of the children as you go along (eg 'Esther' reads 'Secret 1', 'Mordecai' reads 'Secret 2' etc).

SECRET 1

1 The Persian queen, Vashti, had made the king angry. So he was looking for a new queen. Lots of beautiful girls were taken to meet the king, and he chose Esther. However, there was something he didn't know about Esther.

2 Give 'Esther' the envelope marked, 'Secret 1'. Ask your volunteer to open it and read it out to the other children.

3 Explain that the Jews were exiles – a captive nation – living in the Persian Empire. So Esther was one of the lowliest in Persian society. But the king didn't know she was Jewish. Her position as queen put her in the best position for standing up for the rights of her people.

SECRET 2

1 Tell the children about Esther's cousin, Mordecai. He had brought Esther up because she was an orphan. He was a kind and highly respected man who had been given an important job in the king's government. Because of his important position, he learnt a secret.

2 Give Mordecai the envelope marked, 'Secret 2'. Ask your volunteer to open it and read out the 'secret'.

3 Explain that Mordecai told Esther the secret and she told the king. As a result, the king's life was saved. The king was very grateful to Mordecai, and this fact is very important later on in the story.

SECRET 3

1 The king made Haman – a Persian – prime minister. Haman was very pleased with himself and expected everyone below him in rank to bow down to him. Everyone did – except Mordecai. He said that he wouldn't because he was a Jew. Jews worshipped God, not men. This made Haman very angry. He decided on a secret plan.

2 Give 'Secret 3' to 'Haman'. Ask your volunteer to open the envelope and read out the 'secret'.

3 Haman decided that he would get rid of all these troublesome Jews. He didn't realise that the queen herself was a Jew.

SECRET 4

1 Mordecai asked Esther to do something to help save her people from extermination by the evil Haman. This is what she did.

2 Give 'Esther' the envelope marked, 'Secret 4' to open. Ask your volunteer to read out the 'secret'.

3 Explain that even though Esther was queen, she wasn't allowed to see the king unless he sent for her. If she did go to him without being invited, the king might order her to be put to death.

So Esther did a very brave thing: she dressed herself in her best clothes and then went to see him, knowing he might order her execution. But he didn't. The king held out his sceptre to her, which meant she was allowed to go and talk to him.

Esther didn't tell the king what she wanted straight away. Instead, she invited the king and Haman to a special party, knowing all the time what Haman was plotting and what she was going to do. After the first party, Esther invited them to another party. The king of course was very pleased with Esther, and intrigued as to why she was going to all this trouble.

SECRET 5

1 Meanwhile Haman was still feeling very angry with Mordecai. Haman's wife suggested to Haman that he'd feel much more relaxed about the special party, with the king and queen, if he got rid of Mordecai.

2 Give 'Haman' the envelope marked, 'Secret 5' to open. Ask your volunteer to read out the 'secret'.

3 But the king didn't know about Haman's plan to hang Mordecai.

SECRET 6

1 The king remembered that it was Mordecai who had saved him from the assassination plot and he made some secret plans for Mordecai, too.

2 Give 'the king' the envelope marked, 'Secret 6' to open. Ask your volunteer to read out the 'secret'.

3 When the king told Haman he wanted to honour someone very much, Haman thought it must be him! He suggested that the king should arrange a big parade for the man he wanted to honour. Imagine Haman's horror when he discovered it was Mordecai – the man he was going to hang – that the king wanted to reward.

SECRET 7

1 Now it was time for the last part of Esther's secret plot.

2 Give 'Esther' the envelope marked, 'Secret 7' to open. Ask your volunteer to read the 'secret'.

3 At the second party Esther held for the king and Haman, she told the king about Haman's plan to kill all her people, the Jews. The king found out about his plan to hang Mordecai as well. He was very angry with Haman and ordered that he should be hanged on the gallows, instead.

4   As a result of Esther's brave and dangerous secret plotting, she had saved her people from extermination.

Conclusion

1   Tell the children that Esther and her cousin, Mordecai, had another secret you haven't talked about yet. It's a secret that we can all share.

2   Whisper the last 'secret' to a child at the end of the front row and to a child at the end of the back row. Ask the children to pass the secret on, whispering it to each other. Ask them to stop when both ends of the 'Chinese whisper' meet in the middle. Ask the two children who were the last to receive the 'secret' to tell everyone what they think it is. The answer should be:

They knew God was with them.

3   Talk about the fact that Esther and Mordecai knew God was with them and had given them the very special job of saving the lives of thousands of people.

4   Conclude by saying that we also can share this secret; we can know that God is with us and wants to help us to live the right way, even though that isn't always easy.

Time of quiet

Invite the children to join in the following prayer by saying, 'amen' at the end, if they'd like to:

'Help us, Lord, to know that you are with us. Please help us – like Esther – to live your way, even when it isn't easy. Amen.'

Song suggestion

- The journey of life, 45, *Come and Praise 1* and 468, *Junior Praise 2*

20 RECORD BREAKERS!

Aim: To show that it pays to persevere when things are difficult – and God will help us to do that.

Bible base: John 5:2-8 – the healing at the pool.

You will need:

* A copy of the latest version of *The Guinness Book of Records**
* The largest apple you can get (eg a Bramley)
* A sharp knife
* A fabric tape measure (it's important that it's flexible)

Presentation

Introduction
1 Share a personal story with the children about a time when you needed to keep going (persevere) to succeed (eg learning to drive, doing a long walk or climb, completing a long piece of craft work like a piece of knitting or making a model).
2 Show the children an up-to-date *The Guinness Book of Records*. Briefly tell them about some interesting records that demonstrate perseverance (eg polar explorers, ironing, balancing golf balls etc).

Record breakers
1 Tell the children that one of the most amazing records in this book concerns an apple. The record is for the longest, continuous piece of apple peel.
2 Produce your large apple. Tell the children that you are going to try to break that record today in the assembly. Bring out your sharp knife and start to peel. The children will usually watch transfixed and very quiet while you attempt to peel a very thin, very long ribbon of apple peel. Resist requests from the children who will want to have a go, but a teacher or member of

the kitchen staff could be encouraged to join in.

3 When your record attempt has finished, ask one or two children to help you measure your apple peel.

4 Tell the children that *The Guinness Book of Records* gives the record as 52.51 metres established by Kathy Wafler in USA on 16th October, 1976 (it was a very large apple!). This record was still current as of January 1996. Announce the result of your record attempt. Respond appropriately to your success or failure.

5 Comment that it takes a lot of time, patience and practice to achieve a record like that. The amazing apple peeler in the USA must have thought it was worth it. If we want to achieve something special, then we must not give up, but keep on going.

Tell the story
1 Tell the story of the man at the pool (John 5:2-8) simply. You could ask some of the children to act it out as you do so.
2 Emphasise that the man kept on trying to reach the pool, but kept on being beaten. But the man knew what he wanted to achieve (to get well), and Jesus helped him to do it.

Application
1 If we want to live God's way, we will face obstacles and difficulties and sometimes will feel like giving up. We need to be patient and to keep going. The end result is worth it.
2 We can help each other, by encouraging our friends to keep going when things are difficult for them.
3 Just like Jesus helped the man at the pool, he wants to help us to keep going (persevere) when things are difficult.

Song suggestion

* One more step, 188, *Junior Praise 1* and 47, *Come and Praise 1*
* Be bold, 14, *Junior Praise*

21 I CAN'T!

Aim: To show that God never gives up on us. No matter how much we fail him, he will help us to succeed.

Bible base:

John 18:15-18,25-27 – Peter's denial;
John 21:15-19 – Peter with Jesus after the resurrection;
Acts 2-4 – examples of Peter's successful leadership of the early Christians.

You will need:

*   Juggling balls
*   *The Book of Heroic Failures* by Stephen Pile*
*   2 sets of cards for the Bible quiz (as described below)
*   Simple pictures of Peter's life – draw on OHP acetate
*   Picture of 'gloomy face' (as illustrated), copied on to a large piece of card or OHP acetate
*   OHP – if you choose to copy the 'gloomy face' on to an acetate

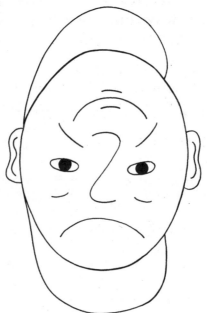

Preparation

* Prepare the cards for the Bible quiz as follows. These have to be big enough for all the children to see. Use large, clear writing. You don't have to use all of these:

SET 1	SET 2
Sarah	Laughed at God
Moses	Killed someone
David	Took someone else's wife
Hannah	Had no children, felt a failure
Peter	Denied he knew Jesus
Thomas	Doubted that Jesus had risen from the dead
Jonah	Ran away from God

* Draw/copy the gloomy face on to card or OHP acetate.
* Prepare the pictures of Peter's life.

Presentation

Introduction
1 Bring out the juggling balls. Tell the children you are going to do some juggling. Even if you can, pretend you can't! The idea is to demonstrate a personal failure.
2 Ask for a couple of volunteers to try as well.
3 Make the point that we all fail at something – and it can make us feel terrible.
4 Give a few brief examples of failure. There are plenty of funny ones in Stephen Pile's *Heroic Book of Failures*.
5 Display the 'gloomy face'.

A Bible quiz
1 Ask for some volunteers, depending on the number of cards you decided to use.
2 Give half of your volunteers one of the name cards each. Give the others the cards with those characters' failures written on. Ask the children to hold up their cards so that everyone else can see, and to stand across the front of the 'stage' area.

3 Ask the rest of the children if they can help you match the name of each character with his or her 'failure' (eg Peter denied that he knew Jesus).

4 Comment that although all these characters failed in some way, they all did great things for God.

Focus on Peter

1 Briefly tell the story of Peter. Show the pictures you have prepared. Emphasise the failure of his denial of Jesus and his despair; how Jesus went out of his way to show Peter that he was forgiven; then how Peter changed; and the success of his work for God.

2 Turn the 'gloomy face' upside down to make it a 'smiley face'. God can bring success out of our failures.

Conclusion

1 Jesus never gives up on us and he wants to help us.

2 Peter went on to write some of the books of the New Testament which we still read in the Bible, today. There he talks about, 'a living hope'. Peter learnt, and God wants us to know, that we are not 'total failures'. He can give us hope and help us to live for him.

Song suggestions

- O Lord, all the world belongs to you, 39, *Come and Praise 1*
- I'm going to shine, shine, shine, 392, *Junior Praise 2*

* *The Guinness Book of Records*, Guinness Publishing Ltd.
* Stephen Pile, *The Book of Heroic Failures*, Futura.

MEET JESUS

22 MEET JESUS!

Aim: To show that, whatever we are like, Jesus cares about us.

Bible base: Mark 10:13-16 (Simon), Mark 7:24-30 (Rachel).

You will need:

- Two large, clear labels, which you can hang on volunteers 'Simon' and 'Rachel'.
- Two large pieces of card. On one side of each card is written: 'Does matter'. On the other side is written: 'Doesn't matter'.
- A card with the word, 'Aah!' written on it in large clear letters.

Preparation

- Rehearse telling the story along the lines of the outline below. Think particularly about how the participation of the children will work.

Presentation

Introduction

1 Tell the children that the Bible tells us about many people who met Jesus. Today you are going to be thinking about two children who met him. The Bible doesn't tell us their names, so you're going to call them 'Simon' and 'Rachel'.

2 Ask for two volunteers to come to the front. Call one of them 'Simon' and the other 'Rachel'. Put the appropriate labels on each of them and ask them to stand one on either side of you.

3 Tell the rest of the children that you are going to need their help, as well, in telling the story. You want them to say, 'Aah!' when they see the sign. Show the sign and give them a practice.

Simon and Rachel

1 MEET SIMON
- Explain that Simon was a young boy when he met Jesus. In Bible times, people thought that children weren't important. When Simon was twelve, then everyone would think of him as a man and treat him as someone important. But he wasn't twelve yet, he was still only a boy. So nobody thought he mattered very much.
- Give Simon the card to hold up, with the words, 'Doesn't matter' showing.
     (Hold up audience response card: 'Aah!')

2 MEET RACHEL
- Tell the children that Rachel was young, too, like Simon. But there was another reason why people thought she didn't matter. Rachel wasn't a Jew. Her mum came from another country – Syria. In Bible times, the Jewish people thought that only other Jews were important. So nobody thought that Rachel and her mum mattered very much.
- Give Rachel the card to hold up, with the words, 'Doesn't matter' showing.
     (Hold up the audience response card: 'Aah!').

3 SIMON'S STORY
- Tell the children that Simon went with his mum and dad to hear Jesus speaking. They listened for a long time and then his mum and dad and some other parents took their children to meet Jesus. But before they could reach Jesus the disciples (Jesus' special friends) stopped them. The disciples thought that children didn't matter, so they told the children and their parents to go away.
- Say, 'Poor Simon.'
     (Hold up the audience response card: 'Aah!').

4 RACHEL'S STORY
- Tell the children that Rachel had become very ill and nobody could make her better. Her mum had heard about how Jesus

had made other people better when they were ill, so she went to ask Jesus for help. When Rachel's mum found Jesus, she was crying very loudly as she was very unhappy. The disciples could see that she wasn't a Jew, so they thought she didn't matter very much. They told Jesus to send her away because she was making too much noise.
* Say, 'Poor Rachel.'
  (Hold up the audience response card: 'Aah!').

5 SIMON AND JESUS
* Explain to the children that, when Jesus saw the disciples telling Simon and his parents to go away, he told the disciples off! Then Jesus spent time with Simon and the other children. Jesus knew that Simon was important and that he did matter.
* Turn Simon's card over to show the words, *'Does matter'.*

6 RACHEL AND JESUS
* Tell the children that Jesus didn't send Rachel's mum away either. Instead, he asked her what was wrong and then told her he would make Rachel better. When Rachel's mum got home she found Rachel lying on her bed – well again! Jesus knew that Rachel and her mum came from another country, but he still thought they were important and that they did matter.
* Turn Rachel's card over to show the words, *'Does matter'.*

Conclusion
1 Conclude by saying that Simon and Rachel both found out that Jesus cared about them – even though other people thought that they didn't matter.
2 Tell the children that the Bible says that everyone matters to Jesus – it doesn't make any difference how old you are or what country you come from or whatever you are like. Jesus cares about everyone.

Song suggestions

- Everyone in the whole wide world, 333, *Junior Praise 2*
- A naggy mum, 302, *Junior Praise 2*

23 FORGIVENESS

Aim: To teach that Jesus doesn't give up on us. He's always ready to forgive us and to be our friend.

Bible base: Mark 14: 27-31,43-50,53-54,66-72 – Peter lets Jesus down;
John 21:15-19 – Jesus lets Peter know he's forgiven.

You will need:

- Pictures to illustrate the story of Peter and Jesus. These could either be drawn on OHP acetates or as a story roll. You could use the pictures suggested in 21 *I can't!* on page 82.

Preparation

- Prepare the illustrations for the story. For a story roll, draw large simple pictures on a roll of lining paper or the back of a roll of wallpaper. You need to unroll the pictures as you tell the story.
- Rehearse your telling of the lumberjack story, thinking carefully about how the children will participate.
- Practise telling the story of Peter and Jesus using the illustrations you have prepared.

Presentation

Drama

1 Ask for five volunteers who are good at acting. Tell them they have to be good at acting because they have to convince everyone they are trees. Get them to practise being different types of trees: tall palm trees, spreading chestnuts, stiff triangular firs etc. Tell them that you want them to be a forest of different kinds of trees. Ask them to get into position across the front of the hall.

2 Choose four more volunteers. They are lumberjacks working in the forest. Get them to stand away from the trees and practise chopping with an axe, sawing with a partner etc.

One of the lumberjacks has a bad leg. (Choose one of them.) Ask them to practise walking with a limp.

Now ask the lumberjacks to take up their positions in the 'forest' and get working!

3 Tell the children that all the lumberjacks were working busily in the forest one day, when along came a very fierce bear. (Ask for a volunteer, who can growl fiercely, to come and be the bear.)

4 Continue telling the story. When the lumberjacks saw the bear they ran away and hid behind the trees – all except the one with the bad leg. He fell over. The bear walked round the lumberjack and then bent down and whispered something in his ear. Then the bear walked off (volunteer 'bear' goes and sits down).

5 Tell the children that when the bear had gone, the other lumberjacks came out of hiding from behind the trees. They said to the lumberjack who had fallen over, 'It looked like the bear was talking to you. What did he say?' And the lumberjack with the bad leg replied, 'He said that he didn't think much of my friends who let me down when I was in danger.'

6 End of drama. Applause. Ask your volunteers to sit down.

Think spot

Ask the children:

Have any of you had friends who have let you down?

What did you feel like?
What did you do?
Who would still be friends with someone who let them down?
Who wouldn't stay friends with that person?

Tell the story

1 Tell the story of Jesus being let down by Peter (see Mark 14:27-31,43-50,53-54,66-72). As you do so, illustrate it either with simple pictures displayed on an OHP, or use a story roll (see *Preparation* above).

2 Ask the children:
Who thinks Jesus wouldn't want to be friends with Peter after this?
Who thinks Jesus would say, 'It's all right, Peter, I forgive you even though you let me down'?

3 Compare these answers with the children's answers to the last two questions in the Think spot section: *(Who would still be friends ... ? Who wouldn't stay friends ... ?).*

4 Now tell the rest of the story which took place after Jesus' resurrection (see John 21:15-19). Again, illustrate the story with some simple pictures (OHP acetates or story roll).

5 Ask the children:
So how did Jesus react when his friend Peter let him down?

Conclusion

- God wants us to be willing to forgive others, too.
- Christians believe that Jesus wants to be friends with us. Whatever we do wrong, if we are sorry, he is willing to forgive us and make friends with us.

Song suggestions

- I'm special, 106, *Junior Praise 1*
- Everybody join in singing this song, 332, *Junior Praise 2*
- Make me a channel of your peace, 147, *Come and Praise 2*

Note: See also 10 *Getting rid of your rubbish*, on page 50 and 27 *Mistakes*, on page 98.

24 THE PRICE IS RIGHT

Aim: To show that the most valuable thing in the world is friendship with Jesus.

Bible base: Matthew 13:45-46 – the parable of the pearl.

You will need:

- Pictures of items the value of which volunteers must guess
- A box which has a piece of paper inside, on which is written in large, clear letters, 'friendship with Jesus'
- *The Precious Pearl* by Nick Butterworth and Mick Inkpen* (optional)

Presentation

The price is right
1 Ask for a volunteer.
2 Show them the pictures of different items.
3 Ask them to write down a price for each item. How much do they think each is worth?
4 Then tell the children the real prices.

Talk about
1 Ask the children what things are valuable to them. Emphasise the difference between something which is valuable because of how much it costs, and something which is valuable because of its meaning (give some examples).
2 Show the children the box. Tell them that something is written on a piece of paper inside the box, and that is the most valuable thing in the world for you.

Tell the story
1 Tell the story of the pearl from Matthew 13:45-46. You could use *The Precious Pearl* by Nick Butterworth and Mick Inkpen.

2 Comment that the pearl was the most valuable thing in the world for the man. He gave up everything so that he could have it.

3 Explain that Jesus told this story to show that being a friend of his is the most valuable thing anyone can have.

Conclusion
1 Ask the children:
Can anyone guess what's inside my box?
Encourage suggestions from the children.
2 Open the box and show them the piece of paper on which is written in large, clear letters, 'friendship with Jesus'.

Song suggestions

- Jesus is a friend of mine, 136, *Junior Praise 1*
- Lost and found, 57, *Come and Praise 1*

Note: See also 1 *How much are you worth?* on page 22, which focuses on the value of each person to God; and 12 *Choose life,* on page 56, which focuses on being willing to receive a gift from God, but doesn't reveal what's inside the parcel.

* Nick Butterworth and Mick Inkpen, *The Precious Pearl,* Collins' Picture Lions (HarperCollins).

25 MISSION IMPOSSIBLE

Aim: To show that Jesus can do things which are impossible for ordinary people to do.

Bible base: Luke 8:40-42,49-56 – Jesus raises Jairus' daughter from the dead.

You will need:

*   2 large sheets of newspaper

Preparation

Prepare and rehearse your telling of the story of Jairus. Think carefully about the participation of the volunteers.

Presentation

Introduction
1 Ask for two volunteers who can fold the sheets of newspaper in half, ten times.
2 Watch while they try to do this.
3 Comment to the children that sometimes things sound easy, but they are actually impossible. Whilst other times, things which sound impossible ...

Tell the story
1 Explain to the children that you will need some help from them. Ask for volunteers to act out the parts of Mr Jairus, Mrs Jairus, Miss Jairus etc, as you are telling a story.
2 Tell the story from Jairus' point of view.
3 Emphasise that when Jairus' daughter was very ill, even though the doctor could do nothing for her, the family thought Jesus might be able to help. Once she was dead, Jairus' thought it was impossible that anyone could do anything for her, but – he was in for a surprise!

Conclusion
1 Explain to the children that Christians believe that Jesus can still do 'impossible' things. That's why Christians pray and ask Jesus to help them or others.
2 We can tell him things that we can tell no one else. We can

ask him to help us when we have problems. He might not always give us the answer we want or expect; but – when we pray to Jesus – we can rely on him to work things out for us in a way that is good and right.

Time of quiet

1 Ask the children to close their eyes and to be very quiet.
2 Invite the children, if they would like, to tell Jesus about anything which they are finding difficult at the moment.
3 Finish with a simple prayer like:
   'Thank you, Lord Jesus, for hearing our prayers. Please help us. Amen.'

Song suggestion

* Jesus is greater than the greatest heroes, 66, *The Big Book of Spring Harvest Kids Praise.*

26 YOU ARE INVITED

Aim: To help the children understand that Jesus offers everyone an invitation to get to know him and his Father, God. A Christian is someone who has accepted that invitation and said 'Yes' to friendship with Jesus.

You will need:

* 7 pieces of card, each piece no smaller than 40 x 70cms
* some brightly-coloured wrapping paper

Preparation

1 Prepare invitations as follows:

- On six pieces of card write a popular first name (three boys' and three girls' names). It is important that there is at least one child of each name in the assembly. So, select names that you are fairly certain some of the children will have. Check the ethnic mix of the school and choose names accordingly. Otherwise, some may feel left out;
- Draw an attractive border around the cards with felt-tip pens etc, to make them look like invitation cards;
- Make sure the words are easy to read from a distance;
- On the seventh piece of card, write at the top, 'Jesus invites ...'. Then in big bold letters across the middle of the card write, 'YOU'. Draw a colourful border again. Wrap this invitation up in wrapping paper. Make sure it is fastened in a way which will be easy for a child to open!

2 Before the assembly begins, place the cards in a pile – face down – at the front of the room, where the children can see it. Arrange the names in alternate sex order. Place the wrapped card at the bottom of the pile.

Presentation

You are invited

1 Explain to the children that you have some invitations which will make some of them special for this assembly. Tell the children that there are different names on the invitations. If, when they see the invitation, their name is on it, you would like them to stand up (or put their hand up).

2 Build up the anticipation by asking the children to do a 'drum roll' with their hands on their legs, before you show them each card. Then produce the card.

3 Ask any children who have the name shown, to stand up. Ask everyone else to give them a clap.

4 Ask one of the children who stood up, to come to the front and hold the card.

5 Continue like this with the six cards. Hopefully, someone will stand up for each card. However, if there is no response, just place the card on the floor where someone would have been standing.

6 When the six cards have been given out, ask the rest of the children how they are feeling if their name hasn't been called out.

- Give some examples of other times when, maybe, they have felt left out (eg teams, games, parties etc).
- Tell the children briefly about a time when you felt left out, using any opportunities for humour.

7 Now, tell the children that you have one more invitation left.

- Ask for a volunteer to come and open the wrapped-up invitation.
- Hold the card up. This time they should all stand up!

Application

1 Explain that Jesus came to earth to invite everyone to get to know him and his Father, God.

2 Briefly give some examples from the New Testament of people whom Jesus invited to be his friends (eg Simon Peter, the fisherman; Zacchaeus, the tax collector).

3 Conclude by explaining that it's still the same today. Jesus invites everyone to get to know him and his Father, God. A Christian is someone who accepts Jesus' invitation to get to know him and to be his friend.

Song suggestions

- Put your hand in the hand, 206, *Junior Praise 1*
- Praise him, 40, *Come and Praise 1*

Note: See also 12 *Choose Life*, on page 56 (This assembly focuses on the choice everyone has to make, whether to accept or reject God's gift of life.) and 24 *The price is right*, on page 92, focuses on friendship with Jesus being the most important thing in life.

27 MISTAKES

Aim: To show that Jesus wants to forgive the wrong things we do.

Bible base: Mark 2:1-12 – the paralysed man.

You will need:

- *Mistakes*, a poem by Michael Rosen from his book *The Hypnotiser**.
- A long, thin strip of paper with some of your past 'mistakes' written on it. Include plenty of examples from your child hood.
- 4 strips of brightly-coloured card jointed with paper fasteners. These are to help you tell the story and can be used to form the bed, legs, the house, steps etc. They need to be big enough for all the children to see, but small enough for you

to handle easily (see *Preparation* below)
- 4 flash cards each showing one of: 'Oh!', 'Ooh!', 'Aah' and 'Eh?'
- A piece of card with the word 'Sorry' written on it (optional).

Preparation

1 Prepare the long, thin strip of paper with your 'mistakes' written on it (to look a bit like a typewriter ribbon).

2 Prepare the jointed strips of card and practise making different shapes which will help illustrate the story as you tell it.

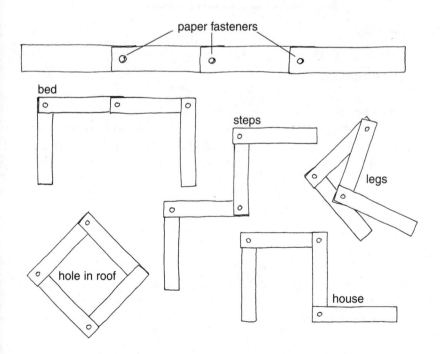

3 Prepare the flash cards.

4 Practise telling the story from memory, using the jointed pieces of card to form legs, bed, the house etc; and the flash cards, for example:

'... the news spread that he was at home ...' (Oh!)

'So many people came together ...' (Ooh!)

'... a paralysed man ...' (Aah)

'... your sins are forgiven ...' (Eh?)

You will soon work out devious ways of using them!

5 Prepare the 'Sorry' card. The letter 'o' could be drawn tear-shaped and slightly below the line of the other letters.

Presentation

Introduction

1 Read the poem *Mistakes* by Michael Rosen. Many schools are familiar with this poem. You might even find the children joining in! Rosen writes about the button on his typewriter which will lift mistakes off the page, leaving them on a long strip which he can look at when the ribbon is full. He realises how embarrassing it would be if he could look at his own mistakes if such a button existed in life.

2 Talk about some of the 'mistakes' you have made, showing the children the long strip of paper with your mistakes written on it. Use any opportunities for humour at your own expense. Make the point that, often, when you do something wrong it is not a 'mistake', but deliberate.

Tell the story

1 Explain to the children that you need their help to tell a story. Tell them that you want them to say the word shown when you hold up a flash card. Give them a practice. When you show them the card with 'Eh?' written on it, explain that they had better say, 'Pardon?' instead, because your mother always said it was rude to say, 'Eh?'

2 Tell the story of the paralysed man (see Mark 2:1-12), using the jointed pieces of card and the flash cards.

3 Focus on Jesus' power to forgive rather than the healing.

Application

1 Explain to the children that the Bible says that Jesus can forgive our mistakes, just as he forgave the paralysed man.

2 Refer back to your own 'mistakes'. Explain what it means to be forgiven. You could use a card with the word 'sorry' written on it, as described above. Use this to introduce a ...

Time of quiet

1 Ask the children to think of some of their 'mistakes'. Invite them to use this time of quiet to say 'sorry' to Jesus. Remind them that they can be forgiven, just like the paralysed man.

2 Say a simple 'sorry prayer' concluding by thanking Jesus for his promise of forgiveness. Tell the children that they can make it their prayer, if they would like to, by joining in with the 'amen' at the end.

Song suggestions

- I'm special, 106, *Junior Praise 1*
- Sorry Lord, 463, *Junior Praise 2*

Note: See also 23 *Forgiveness*, on page 89 and 10 *Getting rid of your rubbish*, on page 50.

* Michael Rosen, *The Hypnotiser*, Lion (HarperCollins).

28 BAD NEWS ... GOOD NEWS

Aim: To show that things are different when we discover that Jesus is with us and he can use the smallest things we do to make things better.

Bible base: John 6:1-13 – the feeding of the five thousand.

You will need:

- A smiling face and a sad face, drawn one on either side of a large circle of card, big enough to be seen clearly by children at the back of the assembly

Preparation

- Draw the faces.

- Practise telling the story of the feeding of the five thousand. Decide at which points you will show the smiling face (good news) and the sad face (bad news). Include them as many times as possible. For example:

'For everyone to have even a little ...' (sad face – bad news),
'... they all had as much food as they wanted' (smiling face – good news),

- Ask friends to post some letters to you which contain 'good news' and 'bad news' (eg a bill, an invitation, a letter from a friend, a charity request etc). The letters should contain a balance of both.

Presentation

Introduction
1 Show the children the letters you have received. Explain you have left them to open in school.
2 Ask for volunteers to come and open them. Ask the children whether they think the contents are 'good news' or 'bad news'.
3 Talk briefly about good and bad news.

Tell the story
1 Tell the children that you need their help to tell the story. When you hold up the smiling face they must say, 'Good news,' and give a thumbs-up sign. When you hold up the sad face they must say, 'Bad news,' and do a thumbs-down sign.
2 Tell the story of the feeding of the five thousand (see John 6:1-13) using the faces. Each time the children say, 'Bad news,' and do a thumbs-down sign, continue with: *'But Jesus was there, and when Jesus is there, things are always different.'*

Application

1 Explain that things are different when we involve Jesus in a situation.
2 Tell the children that Jesus can use the smallest things we can do to make things better – if we let him.
3 Conclude by saying that when we let Jesus help us and use us, 'bad news' can be turned into 'good news' (use the sad and smiling faces).

Song suggestion

- Sometimes problems, 461, *Junior Praise 2*

Note: See also 30 *Loaves and fishes*, on page 108. (This assembly uses the same Bible passage on the harvest theme of sharing.) and 25 *Mission impossible*, on page 93, also makes the point that things are different when we involve Jesus.

29 TRY IT AND SEE

Aim: To help children consider that the claims of the Bible are worth taking seriously.

You will need:

- An OHP and 3 acetates prepared as outlined below
- 3 large cards, written on as shown below
- An inflated balloon and pin
- A chair
- A milk bottle filled with water and *Dettol* (this looks like milk). Replace the top carefully and smooth it over
  Warning: *be careful where you leave this.*

Preparation

- Write on the 3 acetates as follows:
- 'These things are written
- so that you may believe
- in Jesus' (John 20:31).
- Write on the 3 large cards as follows:
  1 This balloon will burst if you stick a pin in it.

2 This chair will take your weight.
3 This is Dettol, so don't try drinking it.

Presentation

Introduction
Display OHP 1. Ask the children for examples of things we see written around us (eg signs, notices etc). Some things we take for granted, others make us curious. Often we don't know whether something is true until we've 'tested' it.

Can you believe it?
1 Display OHP 2.
2 Show the first card. Produce the balloon and pin and get someone to test the truth of the statement.
3 Show the second card. Ask for a volunteer to sit on the chair. The words on the card are true.
4 Show the third card. Ask someone to come and take the top off the bottle, look at it, smell it. They should recognise the smell of *Dettol*. Be ready to stop them drinking, in case they don't!

Try it and see
1 Comment that the three statements were true. There was no trick, but each needed testing.
2 Explain that the words on the OHP are from the Bible. They explain why the Bible was written.
3 **Display OHP 3.** Tell the children that, like many statements, we can choose to ignore it; or we can test it to see if it's true.

Conclusion
1 Conclude by saying that Christians believe that the Bible is true and what it says about Jesus is true. Christians believe that doing what it says helps us to live the right way.
2 Challenge the children to start reading it for themselves. If you feel it is appropriate, you could suggest and show some Bible reading aids for this age group (eg *Let's Go**, *Check it Out!**).

Song suggestions

- God loves you so much, 349, *Junior Praise 2* and 28, *The Big Book of Spring Harvest Kids Praise*
- The baked beans song, 390, *Junior Praise 2*

Note: See also 8 Rules for life, on page 45; 13 *Do what it says*, on page 58 and 37 *Recipe for ... pancakes!* on page 127.

* *Let's Go,* Scripture Union.
Bible reading for the 7-9s, published quarterly.

* *Check it Out!* Scripture Union.
Bible reading for the 9-11s, Funfax format, published quarterly.

SPECIAL OCCASIONS

Harvest

30 LOAVES AND FISHES

Aim: To help children appreciate that all good things come from God. We need to say thank you to him and be ready to share what he gives us.

Bible base: John 6:1-13 – the feeding of the five thousand.

You will need:

- A large lunch-bag or picnic hamper. (It could have a label on it which reads 'My lunch-box' in large clear writing.)
- 5 large, fresh rolls (could be small round loaves), which are almost cut in half – so that they will be easy to break during the assembly. There needs to be enough bread for everyone in the assembly to have a small piece.
- 2 fishes (eg herrings or sprats) or 2 tins of tuna.

Preparation

- Memorise the story so that you can tell it in a way that is entertaining and appropriate to the age group. Think carefully about how you will integrate the 'props', your volunteer with the picnic and the rest of the children into your telling of the story.
- As the children are coming in for assembly, pick a volunteer to look after the 'lunch-box'. Make sure your volunteer understands that they are meant to say, 'yes' when asked if they will share their lunch with the 'crowd'!

Presentation

Tell the story

1 During your telling of the story, refer to the children as if they are the crowd, and to the teachers or some of the older pupils as if they are the disciples (your helpers).

2 Emphasise that the crowd had been with Jesus all day, with nothing to eat. There was no McDonald's nearby! They were very hungry.

3 Tell the children about Andrew finding a small boy with a packed lunch. Ask a 'disciple' (a teacher or older child) to bring your volunteer with the lunch-box to the front (remember to have pre-warned your volunteer that they need to agree to share their lunch!).

4 Bring out the contents, one item at a time, and show them to the children. Talk about the lunch, using any opportunities for humour (eg the size of the 'lunch-box' relative to the size of the child, the size of the bread rolls, the fish or tins of tuna).

5 Emphasise that the boy was willing to share what he had, even though it didn't seem as if it would be much help, considering the size of the crowd.

6 Emphasise that Jesus thanked God for the food, because it is God who provides our food and all good things.

7 Explain that then Jesus broke the bread and asked his disciples to share it out amongst the crowd.

8 Pick several volunteer 'disciples' (teachers or older children). Break the loaves in half and give them to your helpers to distribute evenly amongst the children. Then ask the children to share their piece of bread with those around them, so that everyone gets some. Make sure that all the children have at least a small piece. Tell them they can eat their bread.

9 Explain that maybe you won't share out the fish in assembly, for obvious reasons. It might be smelly and messy!

10 Continue with the story. Explain that what Jesus did was a miracle: five rolls wouldn't normally feed 5,000 people! And everyone in that crowd got – not just a tiny piece – but as much as they wanted. There was even lots left over.

11 Conclude: everyone was better off because the boy was willing to share the little he had.

Application

It's harvest time. That means it's ...

- a time for remembering that the good things we have come from God;
- a time to say 'thank you' to God;
- a time to remember that we should be ready to share the good things we have, because that makes things better for everyone.

A time of quiet

- Ask the children to close their eyes and think about all the good things they have. If they would like to, they could say, 'thank you' to God for what he has given them.
- Then ask the children to think about what they could share with others, today. Again, if they would like to, they could ask God to help them to do it.

Song suggestions

- Thank you, Lord, 32, *Come and Praise* 1
- 5,000+ hungry folk, 16, *Ishmael's Family Worship Songbook*

Note: This assembly idea could be adapted to focus on the theme of sharing. See also 28 *Bad news ... good news*, page 102. This assembly uses the same Bible passage with a different focus.

—————Remembrance Day—————

31 HEROES

Aim: To help children understand more about the meaning of Remembrance Day – and especially that Jesus is the greatest 'hero' of all.

You will need:

- OHP, acetates and pens.
- Object clues (eg a toy phone box for Superman) to help children guess several current fictional heroes, for example: Superman, Batman, Spiderman, Power Rangers.
- Outline of Superman on an OHP acetate.

Presentation

Talk about heroes

1 Show the children various clues, one at a time. They have to guess who the hero is.

2 Ask the children for other suggestions of 'heroes'. Write and display them on an OHP acetate.

3 Display the OHP acetate outline of Superman. Ask the children what qualities they think make a hero. List their suggestions inside the Superman outline.

4 Explain that as well as made-up heroes, like the ones you've been talking about, there have been many real-life heroes. Ask the children if they can think of some. What are some of the characteristics that have made those people heroes? (eg helping other people, being unselfish, fighting for what's right, courage etc.)

Talk about Remembrance Sunday

1 Ask the children:
   Does anyone know what special day it is on Sunday?
   Who or what will we be remembering on Sunday?

2 Explain:

* It is a day for remembering the people who put their lives at risk and died in the wars, so that people like us could live in freedom. They are heroes.
* It is a day for thinking about the greatest hero ever. Ask the children:
  Does anyone know who that is?
  (Answer: Jesus)

Jesus – the greatest hero

* Jesus was the greatest hero of all time. He did amazing things (eg healed the sick, raised the dead, was kind, unselfish, stood up for the rights of others etc). And he gave his life for us.
* Unlike other heroes, he came back to life. He is alive today and wants to help us live the way he showed us.

Time of quiet

* Invite the children to spend a few moments in silence think ing about any real life heroes they know of. Maybe one of their grandparents fought in the last war.
* Then ask them to think about Jesus – the hero we remember especially on Sundays – and all he did to show us the right way to live.
* If appropriate, you could end with a prayer thanking God for Jesus and asking his help to live the way Jesus showed us.

Song suggestion

* Jesus is greater than the greatest heroes, 66, *The Big Book of Spring Harvest Kids Praise.*

Christmas

32 JESUS – GOD'S GIFT TO YOU

Aim:
To help children understand that Jesus is the greatest Christmas gift, and to think about what they can give to him.

You will need:
- Several parcels – different shapes and sizes – gift-wrapped for Christmas.
- Put something inside each parcel which the children will associate with Christmas, for example: a Father Christmas toy/decoration, a mini Christmas tree, decorations, a mince pie, a Christmas card etc.
- A large box with 'Jesus' written on the outside, in letters which are big enough for all the children to see.

Presentation

What's the connection?
1 The parcels should be placed so that they are visible to all the children.
2 Ask for volunteers to come to the front to open the parcels one at a time. Make sure that the 'Jesus' parcel is kept on one side and not opened.
3 Ask the children to show everyone what's in the parcel they have opened.
4 When all the parcels (except the 'Jesus' one) have been opened, ask the children:
   What is the connection between the things which were in the parcels?
   (Answer: Christmas)
   Is there something or someone we've left out of Christmas?
   (Answer: Jesus)

5 Show the children the 'Jesus' parcel.

The best gift

1 Explain to the children that Christmas is made up of many different things, but sometimes we forget that the real meaning of Christmas is Jesus – God's special gift to us. Without Jesus there would be no Christmas.

2 Hold up the 'Jesus' parcel. Point out that it is unopened. Tell the children that Christians believe that Jesus is the best Christmas present. Ask the children:

So what do we need to do to this parcel?

(Answer: Open it and find out what's inside.)

3 Tell the children that the best way to find out what Jesus has to offer is to check him out for ourselves. Ask the children:

Can you think of some people in the Christmas story who did that?

(Answer: The shepherds)

4 Explain that the first Christmas there were some very important people who understood that Jesus was God's special gift to the world. They brought him gifts. Ask the children:

Who were they?

(Answer: The wise men)

What did they give to Jesus?

(Answer: Gold, frankincense, myrrh)

Think spot

1 Ask the children, as they think about all the exciting presents they hope to receive this Christmas, to try to remember that the best Christmas present of all is Jesus – God's gift to them. Encourage them not to leave God's gift unopened, but to check it out for themselves.

2 Remind the children about the wise men who brought gifts to Jesus because they knew he was special. Ask the children:

What could you give him?

3 Explain that, of course, we can't give him a party or wrap up a present to give to him, but there are things we can do for him. Ask the children for suggestions (eg being grateful and thanking God, sharing, helping other people, giving presents to others etc).

A time of quiet

Ask the children to think about what they could give to Jesus this Christmas.

Song suggestion

* Crackers and turkeys, 327, *Junior Praise 2*

Note: See also 34 *The best present*, on page 120.

33 HAPPY BIRTHDAY, JESUS!

Aim: To help children understand that Christmas is special because it's about a very special baby.

Bible base:
Luke 1:31-32 (Mary);
Matthew 1:21,23 (Joseph);
Luke 2:11-12 (Shepherds);
Matthew 2:2 (Wise Men).

You will need:

* 4 large envelopes
* 4 large pieces of paper
* some examples of birth announcements from local newspapers

Preparation

* Write in large, clear letters on the outside of the envelopes as shown in the illustration below:

- On four large pieces of paper, write the following and then put each 'letter' inside the appropriate envelope:

  1 He will be called the Son of the Most High God (Mary's envelope)

  2 You will name him Jesus – he will save his people (Joseph's envelope)

  3 Your Saviour was born – Christ the Lord (the Shepherds' envelope)

  4 The baby born to be the King (the Wise Mens' envelope).

- Before the assembly starts, give out the envelopes to four children.

Presentation

Introduction

1 Ask the children:

Does anyone have a new brother or sister?
Is anyone expecting one?

2 Explain to the children that when a baby is born, the parents want to tell their family and friends all about it: whether the baby is a girl or a boy, the baby's name, how much she/he weighs etc. They might phone their friends up, or they might write a letter. Some families place a birth announcement – a bit like these (show examples) – in their local newspaper. All this happens, of course, *after* the new baby has safely arrived.

3 Tell the children that, at Christmas time, Christians think about the birth of the most important baby ever born – Jesus. Like other babies, there were announcements about his arrival in the world too. Unlike other babies, birth announcements about Jesus appeared *before* he was born!

The four envelopes

Mary

1 Ask the child who has Mary's envelope to come to the front and hold up the envelope.

2 Explain that, before Mary knew she was going to have a baby, an angel called Gabriel came to tell her about Jesus. Tell the children and explain Gabriel's message (see Luke 1:31-32).

3 Ask the child to open the envelope and to hold up the 'birth announcement' which they will find inside.

4 Comment and recap that even before Mary knew she was pregnant, she knew she was going to have a baby boy and that he would be God's Son.

Joseph

1 Ask the child with Joseph's envelope to come to the front and hold up the envelope.

2 Explain that Joseph had a dream in which an angel spoke to him. Tell the children the angel's message (see Matthew 1:21).

3 Ask the child to open the envelope and hold up the 'birth announcement'.

4 Comment that Joseph was probably reminded by the angel's message of another name for this special baby. One of the prophets (God's messengers) in the Old Testament had written that the baby would be called 'Immanuel' which means, 'God is with us' (see Matthew 1:23). So Joseph knew two special names for the baby.

The Shepherds

1 Ask the child with the Shepherds' envelope to come to the front and hold up the envelope.

2 Explain that some shepherds working out on the hills near Bethlehem had a visit from angels, too. Tell and explain to the children what the angel said to the shepherds (see Luke 2:11-12).

3 Ask the child to open the envelope and hold up the, 'birth announcement'.

4 Comment and recap that the shepherds knew – even before they had seen this baby – that Jesus would be the 'Saviour' for his people. They even knew what the baby would be wearing and that he wouldn't be sleeping in a cot!

The Wise Men

1 Ask the child with the Wise Men's envelope to come to the front and hold up the envelope.

2 Explain that the Bible describes the Wise Men as, 'men who studied the stars'. Whatever they were, they had discovered that a very special baby was about to be born. Tell the children what the Wise Men said about him (see Matthew 2:2).

3 Ask the child to open the envelope and hold up the, 'birth announcement'.

4 Comment that, when the star had led the Wise Men to the place where Jesus was born, they presented him with very special gifts. This was because they knew that he was no ordinary baby but 'the King'.

Conclusion

1 Ask your four volunteers to hold up the 'birth announcements'.

2 Tell the children that the Bible teaches us that Jesus is the most important baby ever born. Recap the 'birth announcements':

- he is the Son of God
- he is 'God with us'
- he came to save us
- he is the King.

3 Jesus was a very special baby – and that's why Christmas is special.

A Christmas challenge

Tell the children that you hope they will all have a very happy Christmas Day. Then say that you have a Christmas challenge for them:

> *See if you can remember to say three words when you wake up on Christmas morning: HAPPY BIRTHDAY, JESUS!'*

Song suggestions

- This child, 480, *Junior Praise 2*
- Mary had a little baby, 164, *Junior Praise 1*
- Mary had a baby, 123, *Come and Praise 2*

34 THE BEST PRESENT

Aim: To help children understand why Christians celebrate Christmas.

You will need:

- 3 glasses of water
- 3 party hats
- 1 'king size' *Mars* bar and 2 'party size' *Mars* bars

Presentation

Introduction
1 Tell the children that as Christmas is a time for fun, parties and presents, you thought you should all have some fun now.
2 Ask for three volunteers to play a game.

The game
1 Ask the volunteers to put on party hats.
2 Explain to the children that you are going to have a competition. Each competitor, in turn, must gargle 'Rudolph the Red-nosed Reindeer' (or another well-known Christmas song of your choice).
3 Ask a teacher (or the children) to say who they think did it best.
4 Award the winner a prize (a 'king size' *Mars* bar).
5 Ask the children to applaud the winner.
6 Then give the 'party size' *Mars* bars to the other two competitors. Explain that although they didn't win the competition – so they don't deserve a prize – you are still going to give them a present. After all it is Christmas!

Application
1 Comment that everyone thinks about having fun and receiving presents at Christmas.

2 Tell the children that Christians celebrate at Christmas-time the greatest present ever given by God to the world – Jesus. God gave him to show how much he loves us.

3 Jesus is a gift God wants to give to everyone, whether we 'deserve' it or not.

Time of quiet

Think about the happiness that the presents you give will bring to the people who receive them.

Think about God's present of Jesus to you. What could you do to say 'thank you' to God for his present?

Song suggestions

- Christmas isn't Christmas, 322, *Junior Praise 2*
- Come and join the celebration, 323, *Junior Praise 2*

Note: See also 32 *Jesus – God's gift to you,* on page 113.

—————————— *New Year* ——————————

35 NEW YEAR DRAWER

Aim: To help children understand that we need to get rid of the bad things in our lives (the rubbish), before we've got room for New Year's resolutions (a fresh start with God).

You will need:

- An old drawer full of junk: odd shoes, broken make-up, empty bubble bath bottle, broken tape/CD box, out-of-date clothes etc. Include some items which will make the children laugh
- A bag containing some of 'your' Christmas presents
- A large black, plastic, rubbish bag

Presentation

1 Ask the children about the Christmas presents they received.
2 Ask for a volunteer to come to the front to hold a bag of 'your' presents. Show the children your presents, one at a time, making use of any opportunities for humour at your own expense.
3 Explain to the children that now Christmas is over and it's the New Year; it's time to tidy up and put your presents away. Tell the children that you hope they won't mind, if you start now.
4 Bring out the drawer full of junk. Make sure it is visible to the children. Start to pile your presents on top. But the drawer is so full, the presents won't fit.
5 Comment to the children that there is obviously a problem. Ask them what they think you should do. Help the children, as necessary, towards the answer: *You need to take out the rubbish before*

the new things will fit in.

6 Ask for another volunteer to come to the front and hold out the black rubbish bag for you. Go through the items in the drawer, making use of any opportunities for humour. Put each, in turn, in the rubbish bag.

7 When the drawer is empty, tell the children that now there is room for all the new things. Put your presents in the drawer.

Application

1 Ask the children if they celebrated the New Year. Did any of them make New Year resolutions? Ask for examples.

2 Comment that the trouble with New Year resolutions is that they are hard to keep. They sometimes don't seem to fit into our lives – perhaps because there's a lot of rubbish (eg bad habits, unkind thoughts, temper) in our lives already. We need to clear out the rubbish first – just like the drawer and the new presents.

3 Christians believe that, even though it's hard to do it on your own, you can do it with God's help. We need to tell God that we're sorry for the wrong things we do (ie get rid of the rubbish). Then he will forgive us and, if we ask him, help us to live the right way.

Time of quiet

Ask the children to close their eyes. Tell them that if they like, they could make a New Year resolution now. They could:

- Tell God they are sorry for the things they keep on doing wrong (eg losing your temper, telling lies, being unkind to someone etc).
- Ask God to help them to do what's right this coming year.

Song suggestion

- Jesus is the living way, 67, *The Big Book of Spring Harvest Kids Praise.*

36 A NEW YEAR'S REVOLUTION

Aim: To help children understand that being a Christian is not simply about turning over a new leaf – like making lots of New Year's resolutions. It's about a new life.

Bible base: Mark 10:17-27 – the rich young ruler.

You will need:

- Washing line
- 20 pegs
- 2 sets of letters, each of which include the letters to spell the word 'resolution', plus a selection of extra letters, written clearly on sheets of paper or thin card
- The letter 'V' kept separate from the above

Preparation

- Prepare ten quiz questions (see below). The first letter of the answer of each question should spell the word 'resolution'. Use simple, factual questions.
- Prepare and memorise your own re-telling of the story of the rich young ruler.
- Before the assembly begins, fix up the washing line with pegs across the front of the room where the assembly is to take place. Make sure all the children will be able to see it.
- Place the two sets of letters on two separate tables.

Presentation

Quiz
1 Ask for four volunteers to be two teams of two people.
2 Explain the quiz:
   • There will be ten questions.
   • You will tell them the number of the question, but the

questions will not be asked in order.

• As soon as they know the answer to the question, they must find the first letter of the answer from their pile of letters, and peg it to the appropriate peg on the washing line. (For example: Question 4: *What word is the name of a fruit and a colour?* (Answer: *Orange*) The teams must peg the letter 'O' on the fourth peg.)

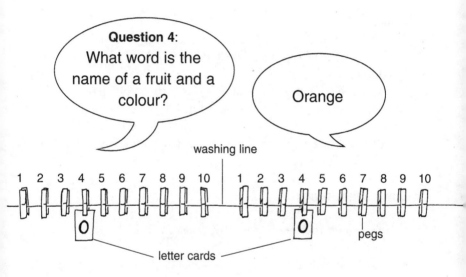

• The first team to do it correctly, wins the round. (Ask a teacher to keep the score.)

3 When the quiz is completed, the word 'resolution' should be on the line twice.

4 Check with your score-keeper which side has won and congratulate the winners.

New Year's resolutions

1 Talk to the children about making New Year's resolutions and how difficult it is to keep them. Give some examples. Ask the children for examples.

2 Explain that some people think that being a Christian is about trying hard to be good and doing the right thing. But it's not.

Tell the story

Tell the story of the rich young ruler, emphasising that he *thought* he was a good person (after all, he kept God's rules, didn't he?) – but he needed to change on the inside. Sadly, he wasn't willing for that to happen.

Conclusion

1. Put the letter 'V' in the place of the letter 'S' in the second word on the washing line. The second word should now read, 'revolution'.

2. Explain to the children that this is the choice we have:
  • 'Resolution' (I'll try my best – but I'll probably fail.)

or

  • 'Revolution' (I want to ask God to change me – he can make me good.).

Song suggestions

• Jesus, send me the helper, 409, *Junior Praise 2*
• Spirit of God, 63, *Come and Praise 1*
• Make me a channel of your peace, 147, *Come and Praise 2*

Note: See also 18 *How to be a frog,* on page 71. This assembly outline is based on the story of Nicodemus and also focuses on the theme of being changed by God.

Lent

37 RECIPE FOR ... PANCAKES!

Aim: To help children understand that living God's way is best.

Bible base: Exodus 20:1-17; Matthew 5-7; John 13:34; 1 Corinthians 13:4-7 – how to live God's way.

You will need:

* An adult assistant to help you
* An electric single hot plate
* Ingredients and equipment for making pancakes
* A recipe book by a well-known cook (eg Delia Smith)
* Clothes to make you, and your assistant, look like cooks (eg chef's hat, PVC kitchen apron with appropriate slogan etc)
* A colourful, contemporary edition of the Bible

Preparation

* Rehearse with your assistant in advance.
* Check with the school, first, that they are happy for you to use the hot plate.
* Check that your volunteers don't have food allergies (eg to eggs, dairy food etc) before they sample the pancakes!
* Set up all you need for making the pancakes before the children come in to the assembly hall:
  for the 'chef's' pancakes: measure out the ingredients accurately in advance and place in appropriate containers,
  for your own efforts: leave the ingredients in their respective packets and boxes.
* Try to avoid excessive mess on the floor and offer to clean up after the assembly.

- Make sure that the electric lead from the hot plate is placed where the children won't trip over it on entering and leaving the assembly.

Presentation

Introduction

1 Ask the children if they know what is important about today (Shrove Tuesday, Ash Wednesday). Explain that Ash Wednesday marks the beginning of Lent.

2 Explain that Lent is the period of forty days leading up to Easter. Many Christians use it as a time to prepare for Easter; the time when we remember Jesus' death and celebrate his resurrection. During this time, Christians also think about the forty days and nights Jesus spent in the wilderness. The Bible says that Jesus didn't eat during this time, so many Christians fast during Lent, or at least give up certain foods (eg chocolate).

3 Explain that, many years ago, it became the tradition to use up all the sweet and luxury foods in the cupboard before Lent began. Making pancakes was a way of using up eggs.

4 Tell the children that there is a story of a lady who was still making pancakes when she heard the church bells ringing. She rushed to church, tossing pancakes on the way ... and that's how pancake races began. Refer to any which are happening locally.

5 Explain that you thought you would have a go at making pancakes now. (If it's Ash Wednesday: 'I missed out on making pancakes yesterday and so ...') But admit that you don't know how to make them ...

Making pancakes

1 Your assistant, dressed as a chef with recipe book in hand, appears and offers to show you what to do.

2 You and your assistant each now prepare a bowl of pancake mixture at the same time. Your assistant should make it clear that they are following the instructions in the recipe book exactly, using the measured-out ingredients prepared in advance. You, on the other hand, take no notice of the instructions and add ingredients from the packets in a haphazard

fashion (eg too much salt, not enough milk, eggshell in the mixture etc). All the while you are preparing the mixture, comment on what you are doing, interact with one another in your dialogue and make use of all the opportunities for humour.

3 When the two mixtures are ready, your assistant should cook some of their mixture. Serve and add topping (lemon and sugar etc).

4 As soon as the hot plate is free, you should start cooking your mixture. Serve.

5 Ask for some volunteers to sample the two pancakes. Ask the children what they think of them. Your assistant's pancake should taste wonderful – because they followed the instructions. Yours tastes awful – because you ignored the instructions.

Application

1 Christians believe that the recipe for a good life is not found in a (Delia Smith/other) recipe book (hold up book), but in another book (hold up Bible). The Bible is God's instruction book for living.

2 Ask the children if they can think of some of the instructions in God's book which help us all to know what's right and to be happy. For example:

- don't steal, don't be envious (The Ten Commandments, Exodus 20:1-1.),
- don't give in to anger, be forgiving (The Sermon on the Mount, Matthew 5:21-26, 6:14-15),
- love others (John 13:34; 1 Corinthians 13:4-7).

If we want to be happy and know how to do what's right, we need to listen to what he says in this book.

Song suggestions

- The baked beans song, 390, *Junior Praise 2*
- Jesus is the living way, 67, *The Big Book of Spring Harvest Kids Praise*

Note: See also 8 *Rules for life*, on page 45; 13 *Do what it says*, on page 58 and 29 *Try it and see*, on page 104.

38 GIVE ME STRENGTH

Aim: To teach that God can give us the strength to say, 'no' to temptation.

Bible base: Luke 4:1-13 – Jesus is tempted by the devil in the desert.

You will need:

- A *Cadbury's Creme Egg*
- Weights
- 2 eggs (1 to use, 1 spare!)
- A bowl
- A damp cloth for cleaning hands
- A PE mat (ask if the school will let you use one for the assembly)

Preparation

- Rehearse the egg demonstration in advance to give yourself confidence that it works!

Presentation

Introduction
1 Show the children the *Cadbury's Creme Egg*. Ask the children if they like these. Describe it in great detail, trying to make the children's mouths water.
2 Ask for a volunteer to come to the front. Ask them to unwrap the egg, look at it, smell it etc. But they must not give in to temptation and lick or nibble it. Leave the child holding the egg, admiring it, whilst you continue.

How strong are you?
Talk about strength in each of the following examples:

Weights

1 Show the children the weights. Give them a brief demonstration, pretending that they are too heavy for you. Explain that weights are meant to build up the strength of your muscles.
2 Ask for a volunteer, who knows how to use weights, to come and give a proper demonstration of how to use them.

Gymnastics

1 Ask if any of the children do gymnastics. Ask for a volunteer to come and demonstrate some moves which require strength and balance (eg headstand, handstand, standing with one leg extended etc). Use the PE mat.
2 Talk about the strength of muscles needed to perform these moves.

An egg

1 Ask a volunteer to come to the front and try to break an ordinary egg into a bowl by squeezing the ends between the middle finger and thumb. It shouldn't break if your volunteer is squeezing the ends. It will break if they squeeze the middle. (Caution: don't do this over the school's new carpet!)
2 Take the egg from the child. Break the egg into the bowl by tapping it first on the edge.
3 Talk about the strength of the egg – the result of its shape.

Talk about

1 Focus everyone's attention on the child who is still standing at the front looking after the *Cadbury's Creme Egg* (still uneaten). Ask everyone whether they think the volunteer has been strong.
2 Comment that the demonstrations with the weights, the gymnastics and the ordinary egg were all about physical strength. Sometimes, though, we need inner strength to say 'no' to temptation – like the volunteer with the *Cadbury's Creme Egg*.
3 Talk to the children about the temptation to do wrong. Give some examples (eg the temptation to cheat, to lie, to be unkind to someone etc). Ask the children for some examples.
4 Comment that it can be hard to say, 'no' to temptation, especially when friends are trying to persuade you to join in with

them and do or say something wrong. You need to be strong.

5 Talk briefly about Lent being a time when we remember the temptations of Jesus. Tell the children that, even though it must have been hard, he didn't give in.

6 Tell the child holding the *Cadbury's Creme Egg* that they can eat the egg now and go and sit down.

Conclusion

God wants us to be strong enough to say, 'no' to what is wrong and brave enough to do what is right. Jesus understands that being tempted is hard. He can help us have the strength to say, 'no'.

Time of quiet

Invite the children to join in the following prayer by saying, 'amen' at the end if they would like to:

Dear God, help me to be strong enough to say, 'no' to things that I'm tempted to do wrong today. Help me to be strong enough to do what's right. Amen.'

Song suggestions

- Jesus, send me the helper, 409, *Junior Praise 2*
- I'm going to shine, shine, shine, 392, *Junior Praise 2*

Note: See also 5 *Do what's right,* on page 35.

Easter

39 CROSSES

Aim: To help children think about the meaning of the cross of Jesus.

You will need:

- Hot cross buns
- A sum written in large numbers on a big sheet of card which has the wrong answer. For example:

$$\begin{array}{r} 2 \\ + \ 3 \\ \hline 6 \end{array}$$

- A big Valentine's card with lots of crosses for kisses inside
- A large 'treasure map' with crosses to mark the position of treasure
- A voting card with the names of candidates standing for election and spaces beside the names for the voter's cross. You could invent names which will amuse the children
- Something which represents the cross of Jesus: a picture, a pendant etc

Presentation

Introduction
1 Tell the children that you were walking down the High Street recently (use local details), when you spotted a bakery. Explain that you couldn't resist going to have a look in the window at all the cakes – cream ones, ginger ones, shortbread etc – and then you noticed some of these ...
2 Take the hot cross buns out of their bag and show them to the children.

3 Ask the children:
Does anyone know what these are?
How many of you like these?
How are they different from ordinary buns?

4 Explain that crosses are used a lot in our world and they have many different meanings.

Crosses

1 THE SUM

- Show the children the sum, keeping your answer covered. Ask the children if they can do the sum. Uncover your answer. Ask the children if it's right. It's wrong, of course. Put a big cross next to it.
- Ask the children if their teacher ever puts a cross beside some of their work, perhaps in a maths or spelling test. Ask the children why. Clarify that it means the answer is wrong, you've made a mistake.

2 THE VALENTINE'S CARD

- Show the children the Valentine's card. Ask them if anyone can tell you what it is. Read the words to the children. Point out that at the bottom of the writing there are lots of crosses.
- Ask the children:
Do these crosses mean that someone has made lots of mistakes?
What do they mean?
- Explain that a cross can mean 'love'.

3 THE TREASURE MAP

- Show the children the treasure map. Ask them what it is, who might have one and what the crosses mark.
- Explain that a cross can mean, 'treasure'.

4 THE VOTING CARD

- Show the children the voting card. Explain what it is. Refer to any recent or forthcoming elections.
- Ask the children if anyone knows what you do to vote.

- Explain that you put a cross by the name of the person you want elected.

5 THE CROSS OF JESUS
- Ask the children if they can think of a cross you haven't mentioned yet.
- Show them the cross (picture, pendant etc).
- Explain that Easter is a special time for remembering Jesus' death on the cross.
- If they haven't already guessed, ask the children:
  Does anyone know what the cross on hot cross buns means?
- Tell the children that we can remember the meaning of Jesus' cross by thinking about all the other crosses ...

Conclusion
Hold up the appropriate 'prop' as you talk.

1 The sum: this cross reminds us that we all make mistakes (give examples) which hurt God.

2 The Valentine's card: this cross reminds us that even though we do things wrong, God still loves us.

3 The treasure map: this cross reminds us that God wants the best for us. He wants us to be his friends. Knowing that God is with you is like finding a hidden treasure.

4 The cross: this cross reminds us that Jesus died on the cross, taking the punishment for our 'mistakes', so that we can be forgiven and be God's friends.

5 The voting card: this cross reminds us that we need to say, 'yes' to Jesus, if we want to be friends with him.

Think spot
Ask the children – when they eat a hot cross bun this Easter – to think about the meaning of the different crosses and especially what the cross of Jesus means.

Song suggestion

- Jesus' love is very wonderful, 139, *Junior Praise 1*

40 BREAKFAST ON THE BEACH

Aim: To communicate that Christians believe Jesus came back to life and that he is still alive today.

Bible base: John 21:1-14 – the disciples have breakfast with Jesus after his resurrection.

You will need:

- A balloon
- a permanent marker pen
- 6 large, numbered envelopes containing the following clues:
  - a small boat
  - a small piece of garden netting (to represent fishing net)
  - a cut-out cardboard fish shape
  - a piece of bread
  - a picture of a fire
  - a smiley face (eg a picture, badge, or cardboard circle with a smile drawn on it)

Preparation

- Place the six objects in their respective envelopes. Number them clearly. Hide them around the room where the assembly will take place.
- Learn the story from John 21:1-14 so that you can tell it from memory, using the clues suggested at appropriate moments.

Presentation

Introduction
1 Blow up the balloon.
2 Talk about how sad Jesus' friends were when he died. Draw a sad face on the balloon.

3 Talk about the disciples' sadness and confusion during the time between Jesus' death and resurrection.

Tell the story
1 Explain to the children that you are going to need some of them to help you tell a story.
2 Tell the story from John 21:1-14 dramatically, using the envelope clues as you go along. Invite a child each time to find one of the hidden envelopes (in numerical order), bring it to the front and open it. Ask them to show the 'clue' to the rest of the children. Talk about it and use it to move the story on.
3 Talk about the special breakfast meal, emphasising how happy the disciples must have felt when they realised that Jesus was alive.

Application
1 Explain that Christians believe Jesus is still alive today.
2 Turn the balloon 'sad face' upside down to make a happy face.
3 Explain that, like the disciples, we can feel happy too: because Jesus is alive, we can know that he is with us today.

Song suggestions

• Peter and James and John in a sailboat, 197, *Junior Praise 1*
• Lord of the dance, 22, *Come and Praise 1*

Note: See 21 *I can't!* on page 82, for an example of a sad/smiling face.

—————————— *Pentecost* ——————————

41 HOW DOES HE DO THAT?

Aim: To help children to understand that although we can't see the Holy Spirit, we can see what he does.

Bible base: John 3:6-8 – the Holy Spirit described as wind.

You will need:

- 2 pieces of string which are the same length (about 150cms)
- 2 paper cups
- An empty milk bottle
- A small ball of screwed-up paper which will rest just inside the neck of the bottle
- A rubber glove

Preparation

- Make a hole in the middle of the bottom of each paper cup, so that they will move easily along the string. Thread each cup on to one of the pieces of string.
- Check that the experiment with the ball of paper in the bottle neck works easily. You may need to adjust the size of the paper ball, type of bottle you are using etc.

Presentation

Game
1 Ask for four volunteers to make two teams of two people.
2 Give each pair a piece of string with a cup threaded on it.
3 Tell each pair of children to hold the string taut between them, with the paper cup at one end.

4 Explain that the game is a race. Child A must blow the cup along the string to child B.

5 Encourage all the children to cheer on the contestants. You could divide the audience into two sections, each supporting their own 'team'. Congratulate the winners.

An experiment

1 Explain that you are now going to do an experiment. Lay the bottle on its side on a table and place the paper ball so that it rests just inside the neck of the bottle.

2 Ask the children:

If someone blows into the bottle, will the paper ball go in or out?

3 Ask for a volunteer to come to the front to try to blow the paper ball into the bottle. (It should come out!)

Talk about

1 Talk to the children about the wind. Explain that – just like the children blowing the cups along the string, just like the ball being blown out of the bottle – you can't see the wind, but you can see what it does.

2 Ask if any of the children know what Christians celebrate at Pentecost. Explain that when Jesus went back to heaven, he promised his friends that he would send the Holy Spirit. Then God – the Holy Spirit – would be with them, even though they couldn't see him.

3 Tell the children that the Holy Spirit is sometimes described in the Bible as a wind (eg John 3:6-8). That's because even though we can't see him, we can see the effects of his power.

Hand in glove

1 Place a rubber glove on a table in view of everyone. Announce that the rubber glove will now perform various actions (eg crawl along the table, do a somersault etc). Coax it. Then pretend to get annoyed when it does nothing.

2 Comment that, of course, the glove won't move unless you put your hand inside it.

3 Do so. Announce once again that the glove will now perform various actions. This time your hand obediently crawls along the table etc!

Conclusion

1 Explain that even though we can't see the Holy Spirit, he is at work in the world. Briefly, give a few examples, illustrating that he works through people's lives, changing them and the world for the better.

2 The promise Jesus made to his disciples about the Holy spirit, is for anyone who chooses to be Jesus' friend. Jesus promises to send the Holy Spirit – sometimes called the Helper – to be with them too, to help them live Jesus' way.

Song suggestions

- Jesus, send me the helper, 409, *Junior Praise 2*
- If you climb, 388, *Junior Praise 2*
- Spirit of God, 63, *Come and Praise 1*

End of year

42 ALL CHANGE

Aim: To show that God can help us cope with change.

Bible base: Genesis 11:31 – 12:7 – Abraham sets out from home and settles in a new land.

You will need:

• Clues for the answer 'France'. If you choose another country, you will need different clues as appropriate. For 'France' you could include:
  • a croissant
  • a bottle of French wine
  • some garlic
  • some crêpes
  • a road map of France
  • a beret
  • a packet of French coffee
  • *Ambre Solaire* sun cream etc
  • a bag to put all the clues in (eg a *Le Shuttle* carrier bag if the answer is 'France')

Preparation

Memorise the story of how Abraham left his home (Genesis 11:31 – 12:1-7) and prepare to tell it in a way which highlights the theme of change and how to cope with it.

Presentation

Introduction

1 Bring out your bag of 'props'. Tell the children you have just got back from holiday. (Let them know you are pretending, if you are!) This is a bag that you haven't unpacked yet. Take the items out one by one, commenting as appropriate. Ask the children to guess where you have been.

2 Ask the children:
What's different about France (other country) *compared with the United Kingdom?* (Language, you drive on the right, food etc)
What's the same? (People etc)

3 Tell the children that even though some things were the same, it was also very different. You enjoyed your holiday – trying to speak a different language, the sun etc – but in the end it was good to come home where you could speak English and you were used to everything.

Talk about

1 Talk about the big changes facing some of the children who are about to go to secondary school (eg different buildings, new teachers, new classmates). Refer to other changes that some children might be facing (eg moving house, a new family situation).

2 Comment that although changes can be exciting, they can also be a bit frightening, because we know things are going to be different.

Tell the story

1 Tell the story of God's call of Abraham. Explain that Abraham was an old man and very wealthy when God told him to leave his home. He was to go to a foreign country where he didn't speak the language, where people dressed differently and ate different food. He would live in a tent in the country instead of in a house in the city. God wanted Abraham to go to this strange country because he had great plans for him.

2 Comment that it must have been very difficult for Abraham to leave his home. But he went because he knew that God

would be with him and would help him to cope with all the things which would be different.

Conclusion

Conclude by telling the children to remember, as they face big changes, that God is with them. They are not alone and God has got good plans for them, if they will trust him.

Time of quiet

Ask the children to close their eyes and to think about any changes they are facing. Remind them that God will be with them and wants to help them cope.

Song suggestions

* God was there, 352, *Junior Praise 2*
* One more step, 47, *Come and Praise 1*

Note:

1 See also 17 *God's got plans for you*, on page 67. This assembly also looks at the theme of God having a plan for our lives and being with us in the good times and the bad times.

2 Scripture Union have also published a booklet for children changing to secondary school called *Moving on ...** by Jo Bailey, which works through some of the questions and feelings they may have at this time.

* Jo Bailey, *Moving on ...* , Scripture Union.
  See Resources section, on page 144, for details.

FURTHER RESOURCES AND USEFUL ADDRESSES

Resources

- Jo Bailey, *Moving on ...*, Scripture Union. Booklet for children changing to secondary school. Available singly or in packs of 20 with free teacher's guide.
- Chris Chesterton and Pat Gutteridge, 52 Ideas for *Junior Classroom Assemblies*, Monarch. For use with individual classes and large groups.
- Margaret Cooling, *Assemblies for Primary Schools*, Religious and Moral Education Press (RMEP).
- Margaret Cooling, *Wisdom for Worship*, Stapleford Project Books (ACT). Assemblies based on teaching from the book of Proverbs.
- Joanna Pitkin, *Line up for Assembly*, Scripture Union.Class assemblies for 7-11s.

Further reading

- Emlyn Williams, *The Schools Work Handbook*, Scripture Union.

Songbooks

- *The Big Book of Spring Harvest Kids Praise*, ICC in association with Spring Harvest.
- Geoffrey Marshall-Taylor (compiler), *Come and Praise 1*, BBC Books.
- Geoffrey Marshall-Taylor (compiler), *Come and Praise 2*, BBC Books.
- *Ishmael's Family Worship Songbook*, Kingsway Music.
- Horrobin/Leavers (compilers), *Junior Praise 1*, Marshall Pickering.
- Horrobin/Leavers (compilers), *Junior Praise 2*, Marshall Pickering.
- *Someone's Singing Lord*, A & C Black.

Useful addresses

Scripture Union in Schools, 207-209 Queensway, Bletchley, Milton Keynes, Buckinghamshire MK2 2EB Tel: 01908 856000

Schools Ministry Network, 207-209 Queensway, Bletchley, Milton Keynes, Buckinghamshire MK2 2EB Tel: 01908 856000

Stapleford House Education Centre, Wesley Place, Stapleford, Nottingham NG9 8DP Tel: 0115 939 6270